FORTUNE FAVOURS
THE BRAVE

FORTUNE FAVOURS
THE BRAVE

The Battle of the Hook
Korea 1953

BY
A. J. BARKER

LEO COOPER

First published in Great Britain 1974
Reprinted in this format 2002 by
LEO COOPER
an imprint of
Pen & Sword Books Ltd,
47 Church Street, Barnsley, South Yorkshire S70 2AS

Copyright © A. J. Barker, 1974, 2002

ISBN 0 85052 823 2

A CIP catalogue record for this book is available
from the British Library

Printed in Great Britain by
CPI UK

CONTENTS

ILLUSTRATIONS

FOREWORD

by *Major-General Sir Douglas Kendrew*, KCMG, CB, CBE, DSO,
Commander 29 Inf Bde 1952-53 Korea

I am glad to have this opportunity of writing a short foreword to
Lt.-Colonel Barker's story of the Battle of the Hook that took place
in Korea during the end of May, 1953.

It gives me the chance to pay tribute to a wonderful Brigade
consisting of the 1st Bn The Black Watch, 1st Bn The King's Regiment, 1st Bn The Duke of Wellington's Regiment and the 20th Field
Regiment Royal Artillery, with other supporting arms.

All the Bns played their full part in this battle; however the main
attack fell on the Dukes and their fighting qualities were outstanding.

This battle was unique in many ways. Not since the trench warfare of the 1914–18 war have British forces fought a battle of this
pattern, and it is unlikely that it will be fought again with the advent
of tactical nuclear weapons.

Artillery played more than a major part in the planning of the
defence. Great praise must be given to Lt.-Colonel Geoffrey Brennan who, with his Counter Bombardment officers, executed the fire
plan and so decimated the attacking Chinese that the Infantry
survived the waves of men who tried to overrun this key position.

I must also pay tribute to the National Servicemen that made up
sixty per cent of the Regular Battalions. These young men, mostly
nineteen years old, adapted themselves to the art and hell of war
and played a full part in writing their Regiments' histories. Many of
the platoons were led by National Service officers.

But in writing this foreword to the story of a vital battle, I do not forget the other units and formations in the Commonwealth Division who maintained to the full the highest traditions of British Forces, and thus made us proud to belong to a unique band of men who were fighting to uphold the ideals of freedom.

PREFACE

In the closing stages of the Korean War some twenty divisions were fighting 'in defence of the principles of the Charter of the United Nations' on the 38th Parallel. Of these, one was the Commonwealth Division which held a front separated from the sea to the west only by a division of the United States Marine Corps. The commander of that division had once said in a voice of respect, 'You know, I have the sea on my left flank and the Commonwealth Division on my right, and when I go to bed at night I sleep well because I know that when I wake up in the morning they'll both still be there.'

Two pivotal bastions of defence formed the cornerstones of the Commonwealth Divisional front – the massive Pt 355 ridge, whose peak was so hard that dug-outs on it had to be blasted out with explosives, and Hook ridge. Both features were coveted by the Communist forces, and 'the Hook', that tenuous angled spearhead of a whole stretch of front, saw more British blood spilled on its sides, and a greater concentration of Chinese and North Korean blood on its face, than any battlefield on the Korean peninsula.

In all there were some five battles for possession of the Hook, of which three are remembered. The first was fought on the night of 26/27 October, 1952, by the 7th United States Marine Regiment under most unfavourable conditions. The second and most costly in casualties was fought on the night of 18/19 November, 1952, by the 1st Battalion, The Black Watch, who were also holding the Hook for the prelude to the third battle. This action, the brunt of which fell on the 1st Battalion, The Duke of Wellington's Regiment, stands as the last major feat of arms to have been fought by any British unit. Beside it such actions as Suez or Borneo were very small beer for the units taking part. As a result of it, awards were made of two Distinguished Service Orders and half a dozen Military Crosses and Military Medals. The Third Battle of the Hook was a protracted affair of wiring, mining and bunkering, of mortaring, shelling and air-strikes, and of steady persevering defence by patrols, tunnelling and trench work. It came to a climax on the night of 28/29 May, 1953, when greater concentrations of artillery were brought to bear on a 1000-yard front than at any time since 1918. Several battalions of Chinese were broken on the Hook that night, and 'The Dukes' – mainly National Servicemen from Yorkshire – suffered relatively heavy casualties themselves. But they did not budge, and in the morning they still held the Hook. Fortune had favoured the Brave. At the dawn of a new Elizabethan era, this resounding victory showed the world that the British Lion was not as yet decadent.

PROLOGUE

When the Korean War broke out in 1950 the Western world was ill-informed about Korea. And, although British, Turks, Belgians, Greeks and Frenchmen were soon fighting in its defence beside the more numerous Americans, interest in this conflict rarely went beyond bewildered apprehension that an East-West test of power was going on in a remote and misty land. Coming so soon after the Second World War, the conflict seemed an anticlimax, and leader writers have often referred to it as 'the forgotten war'. In Britain, still grappling with food rationing and power failures and preoccupied with the birth of the Welfare State, the last thing anybody wanted to hear about was a war – even a war sponsored by the United Nations against 'an act of unprovoked aggression'. Britain contributed more military assistance than the score of other countries who supported the United Nations bid to uphold the rule of law. But this was only because it had not yet occurred to anybody that she was no longer a 'Great Power'.

Like the war in Vietnam, the Korean War was the fruit of the American policy of 'global containment'. In 1945, as part of a Russo-American arrangement to accept the surrender of Japanese forces in the country, Korea was divided at the 38th Parallel. In the south the Government of the Republic of Korea – although neither a perfect democracy nor wholly pacific in its temper – was recognized by the United Nations General Assembly as the only valid government in the country. In the North the Soviet-sponsored state known as the 'Democratic People's Republic of Korea' was recognized by the Communist powers.

On 25 June, 1950, North Korean troops crossed the 38th Parallel; four days later they were in Seoul. On this occasion the United Nations acted swiftly, calling for a cease-fire and the immediate withdrawal of the North's forces. When this demand was ignored, American troops under the flamboyant General Douglas MacArthur were sent to support the armies of the South. The first two months of the war were marked by communist victories, and by August the defenders were hemmed in round Pusan. Primarily as a consequence of a daring and successful sea-borne attack on Inchon, MacArthur was back in Seoul by the end of September. Instructed by the U.N. General Assembly 'to secure stability throughout Korea' he now moved across the 38th Parallel in pursuit of the fleeing North Koreans.

India and other Powers had warned the Americans that China would intervene directly if her border were threatened; that what had begun as a police action might then become a world war. Nevertheless MacArthur proclaimed an 'end of the War' push that would, he said, bring the troops 'home by Christmas'. Events soon showed that India had been right. Two hundred thousand Chinese 'volunteers' had been thrown into battle by the end of November, and half a million more were concentrating to move down into Korea; behind them was a human avalanche of millions more. According to the ever-ebullient MacArthur it was an 'entirely new war', and in Washington President Truman told a Press Conference that use of the atom bomb was 'under active consideration'.

In Britain, the public had given only fitful attention to the war-correspondents' stories of Chinese bugles in the dawn, on-rushing Red hordes, and the pathos of the refugees. For most people it was business as usual. The whistles and whooshes

on the newsreels and the headlines telling of attacks and coun-
ter-attacks seemed just one more monotonous element in the
background of the times. Spiralling prices, the recently imposed
charges for National Health spectacles and dentures, Dr Ponte-
corvo, and the complex and disturbing treacheries of Guy
Burgess and Donald MacLean were of far more concern than
the endless battles in Asia. Not until May, 1951 – when the
Gloucesters lost 600 men in their four-day stand at the Imjin
River – did the war really come home to the British. Even then
the news from Korea was hard put to compete with 'Festival
magic' on the south bank of the Thames.

News that the United Nations 'police action' had taken a
new turn did stir some interest. But an announcement that the
Prime Minister was flying to see President Truman reassured
most Britons, and once more it was business as usual.

Mr Attlee returned from his mission; 'MacA' was relieved of
his command, the war lost its momentum. When the troops
drew back to the 38th Parallel the conflict entered a new static
phase, overshadowed by political considerations. Peace feelers
were put out in May and truce negotiations started in July,
1951.

The Communists had failed to overrun South Korea but they
were determined to milk the armistice negotiations of every
conceivable propaganda advantage. So, while the negotiators
argued at Panmunjon, the war dragged on. Both sides reinforced
their positions, and the peninsula was scarred with opposing
trench systems reminiscent of the Western Front in 1916. By
the summer of 1952 a balance of tactical stalemate had been
struck and from then on the fighting was confined to savagely
contested struggles for hills significant to the eventual demarca-
tion line. In May, 1953, these grim battles crescendoed into an
attempt to seize one such hill four miles northwest of the con-
fluence of the Sami-chon and Imjin Rivers. 'The Hook' as it
is called, was the key position in the Commonwealth Division's
sector of the United Nations front. Because it dominated the

ancient invasion route to Seoul its possession was vital, and in the course of the war it had already been the scene of much bitter fighting. This final battle was to be the most bloody engagement of them all.

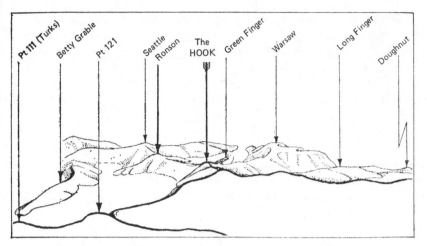

The Hook terrain viewed from the reserve company area

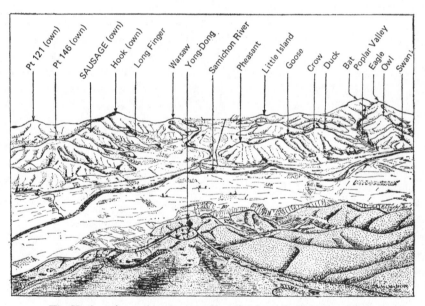

The Hook environs viewed across the valley from the British positions
on the right flank

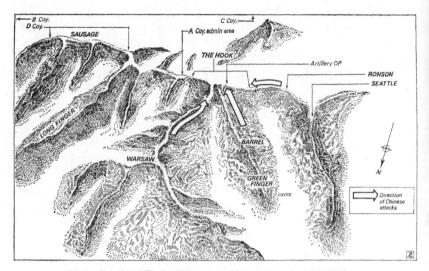

The valley foothills leading up the Hook ridge, showing Chinese
approaches, May, 1953

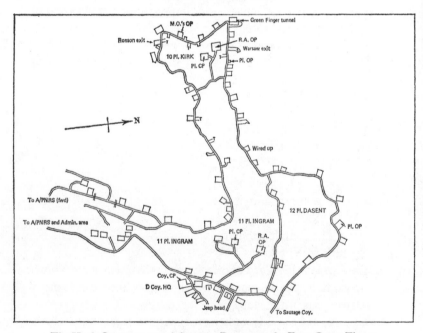

The Hook Company trench layout – Ronson to the East, Green Finger
and Warsaw to the north

I

BATTLE ORDER

Historical experience is written in blood and iron.
                                    MAO TSE-TUNG

Ten o'clock in the morning, a bleak winter morning in the middle of the war. Behind the front in Korea twenty million refugees cowered and shivered in ditches, under bridges and in the ruins of peasant cottages. In Seoul prisoners were lining up to be shot, while the brothel-owners and black marketeers prepared for another day's vice. South of the 38th Parallel United Nations troops lay in their freezing dug-outs waiting for the sudden whistles and the bugle calls which would herald the next Chinese attack.

Ten thousand miles to the west, staff officers gathered in Whitehall to decide on reliefs and reinforcements for the units actively engaged in the battle against aggresive communism. In Korea many factors calculated to lower the morale of fighting men were present, and it had been decreed that no soldier should be required to spend more than a year in that unhappy country. The trouble facing those meeting to decide who should take a turn in Korea was that their choice was strictly limited. In the Crimea the War Office earned a reputation for impenetrable muddle which, many averred, it had since maintained. But there was little scope now for permutations of muddle. Britain had retreated from her great base in India and slashed her forces after the Second World War. In the 1870s, Colonel Cardwell had devised a system for ruling the Empire which depended on seventy-five regiments, each of two battalions – one at home, the other guarding a distant outpost. Since that afternoon in Hiroshima seven years before, however, the second battalions had been declared redundant and relegated to the limbo of 'suspended animation'. Senior officers, nurtured on regimental traditions and the belief that a fighting soldier rates higher in the army's social scale than a technician argued vehemently against the changes. The teeth will be swallowed by the tail, they declared. Technology will solve all the army's problems, the boffins replied. And the politicians agreed. With less red on the map, fewer men would be needed in the proverbial red coats, they postulated. The military system needed to be reorganized and the complex tribal basis of its regiments abolished. Thus is was that when the cold war flared up, and Britain needed the 'old-fashined' kind of soldiers to deal simultaneously with an 'emergency' in Malaya, Mau-Mau in Africa, and the United Nations 'police-action' in Korea, her armoury was embarrassingly depleted.

News that the War Office had 'selected' his battalion for service in Korea was telephoned to Lieutenant-Colonel Ramsay Bunbury immediately the conference in Whitehall broke up. Resources had been reviewed, alternatives considered, and the ramifications of the move discussed; the staff, according to the cliché, had left no stone unturned. By November the Welch Regiment would have spent a year in Korea, and it would have to be the 1st Battalion, The Duke of Wellington's Regiment which took over.

Colonel Ramsay Bunbury was a remarkable man. Slim and of medium height, his face had a rugged yet frail handsomeness, pale and set in firm lines, the expression betokening a sympathy and understanding which was almost as incongruous in this physiognomy as his taste for racing was against his background.

Always faultlessly turned out, he appreciated gracious living but was spartan, particularly in the simplicity of his own diet. His voice was quiet but inspired respect. At the same time he was not a man to suffer fools gladly, and his orders were always obeyed instantly and willingly, however distasteful the circumstances. The news came as as complete surprise; nevertheless the prospect it unfolded did not displease him. Forty-two years old, neither war nor service in the Far East deterred Ramsay Bunbury. In the family tradition he had already seen plenty of both, and the distinctive ribbon of the Distinguished Service Order on his uniform already testified to his gallantry in action. If there was a choice the colonel preferred real war to war games and the nuclear make-believe of training in Germany.

Others under his command were less pleased when the forthcoming move was announced. Many of the officers and most of the senior NCOs had had their fill of war between 1939 and 1945, and of unsettled domestic lives ever since. In December, when the battalion had been posted to Minden, they had breathed a sigh of relief. Now, at long last, they could look forward to a relatively undisturbed and orderly existence in a pleasant corner of Germany, proud of its long connection with England. Some of the families were already comfortably established in the Minden married patch. Others were on the verge of moving – under arrangements which were promptly cancelled as soon as word that the battalion was under orders for Korea filtered across to that branch of Whitehall officialdom, known as 'Q Movements (Married Families Passages)'. Service in the British Army of the Rhine carried a number of perks – being able to buy a new car free of purchase tax being among them. Consequently many of the younger officers had already scraped together or borrowed money, mortgaged their future, and rushed into the purchase of shiny new vehicles. Now, if they sold their car in Germany they lost money; and, because the concessionary period of two years had not expired, if they took it to England the Customs authorities demanded purchase tax.

Up to this time the families who had succeeded in joining their menfolk in Minden were the envy of those wives who were waiting to move. The boot was now on the other foot. Not only did the families in Minden face another upheaval, the majority of them had no permanent homes to which they could return. The wives in England had avoided the tedious problem of packing, unpacking, disposing of the uneconomic bits and pieces at one place and subsequently buying others to replace them, taking the children from one school and settling them in another. And most of them were able to carry on in the same house until the Dukes finished their time in Korea. But many of the women in Germany had nowhere to go back to, at a time when accommodation in post-war Britain was at a premium. As has been the case so often in the past, the problems of the British Army's married men were to exercise the patience of the military authorities.

To cater for the families of the Dukes and other units whose lives had been disrupted by the troubles in the Far East, orders were issued for wartime camps to be hurriedly refurbished and accommodation requisitioned in boarding houses at seaside resorts. At places like Blackpool the Whitehall pundits reckoned the landladies would welcome an influx of paying guests in the off-season. Some did, and most tried to make life a little more bearable for the grass widows in their charge. But the so-called 'family camps' were less of a success. Conditions to which some of the Dukes' women were consigned were cramped and perhaps more suited to the camp followers of the regiment at the time of the Great Duke himself than today's accepted standards of amenities. Army wives no longer expect to queue for their meals in a mess hall with knife, fork and spoon. Moreover they expect privacy. One such camp was commanded by an elderly dug-out major – a dubious alcoholic character of somewhat raffish appearance. Either it had been suggested that his lonely females needed male company or else he was anxious to correct the inhibitions of three hundred full-blooded young sailors at a naval training base just down the road. In any case at weekly dances the lusty matelots were given an opportunity to escape their masculine environment. But what visiting husbands saw of their sallies into female society was sufficient to cause many of the families to be abruptly withdrawn.

What happened to the families was the least of Ramsay Bunbury's problems at this time. His prime concern was to prepare the battalion for war, and the manpower situation was uppermost in his mind. Most of the regiments in Germany were sadly under strength. Rhine Army was counted a 'home' station when it came to considerations of reinforcement and the pressing demands of the world's trouble spots had priority. At this time the Dukes were only about 400 strong, while the war establishment of a first line battalion was 37 officers and 872 'other ranks'. Furthermore a number of officers and senior NCOs were either unsuited or ineligible for active service. In dim and distant Korea there was no place for portly old majors, or sergeants and corporals whose service with the colours was drawing to a close. Many changes were necessary and those who remained had to absorb and weld an influx of newcomers into the battalion before it would be in a position to acquit itself well in the forthcoming campaign.

From the end of February until the battalion actually moved into the line in Korea there was a steady influx of men. (By far the largest contingent was drafted in at Pontefract, where the battalion staged en route from Minden to Pusan.) Meanwhile the personnel branches of the War Office and the Infantry Records office were scrutinizing staff and extra-regimental appointments with a critical eye, and in the ensuing six months the cream of the regiment's officers and senior NCOs were posted to Colonel Bunbury's command.

In Germany the first step was to 're-sort' those who would be going to Korea, and to pack off those whose future was elsewhere. Some reorganization was also necessary. As communist tanks were not a menace in Korea, the Anti-Tank platoon –

considered a vital component of infantry battalions serving in the Rhine Army – was disbanded, its gunners and loaders becoming machine-gunners and mortar men. Similarly the strength of the thirty-three-strong assault pioneer platoon – specialists in explosives and demolition – was halved and the surplus individuals dispersed. But the machine-gun and mortar platoons were boosted. Reports from Korea stressed the worth and importance of both weapons, and Ramsay Bunbury wanted to ensure that his machine-gunners and mortar men should be as expert in their respective roles as training facilities in Germany could make them.

Preparing for the exacting tasks ahead was left entirely to the Dukes' commanding officer. Theoretically the battalion was answerable to Brigadier Freddy Graham until it actually left Minden. But Graham, besides being a colourful and entertaining individual, was an efficient brigade commander who believed in letting a commanding officer have his head. He appreciated the difficulties confronting Bunbury, and the 1st Dukes were given a free hand to get on with whatever form of training Bunbury considered was best.

Because re-sorting, reorganizing and training all had to go on at the same time, the programme pursued in the four months left to the battalion in Germany was always hectic and often haphazard. No principles were propounded as such, but Bunbury was determined his men should be fit for war, not only in the physical training and ball-game sense of the word, but *tough*. In his own experience the dour Yorkshiremen excelled in the art of sticking it out. He knew that, well-led, a new generation of Dukes would fight with as much ferocity as any opponent. But more than dourness would be needed if his men were to grapple successfully with Asiatic peasants, whose background, docility, rigid discipline and unflinching response to orders under the most trying conditions made them such a formidable enemy. Confidence in their weapons had to be instilled in every individual going to Korea. Mental alertness, physical fitness, proficiency and pride: these were the criteria of a professional soldier. And they would be welded by the moral strength that comes from regimental pride.

What goes to make regimental pride is not always easy to define or to weigh. Tradition, history and the individuality of the unit are three of the more important factors. On many occasions when all has seemed lost it has turned the tide of battle. Nothing can replace it, and in common with other regiments Bunbury's officers firmly believed that their unit had something a little extra which the others had not. Virtually all of them fitted into the same general pattern. Despite the fact that Yorkshire is the cricketing county, and the best racehorses are trained there, the Dukes are not known for their cricketing prowess or for the hunting and racing activities of the officers. The Dukes are a rugby playing regiment, and nearly every officer in Bunbury's battalion had made his mark on the rugger field at some time or other. Those who had not done so could box or shoot better than most; the colonel himself was a champion Bisley shot. All enjoyed good living and took part with zest in the robust and harmless diversions indulged in the mess on formal dinner nights. Almost to a man the regular officers emphasized the tremendous influence of public school tradition in what might be described as the upper middle class of the British Army. Non-regular officers – National Service subalterns for the most part – were non-union members, as it were. But they were treated with friendly courtesy and found their brother officers pleasant companions.

Eighty per cent of the troops were National Servicemen – conscripts impressed into an army which had failed to attract a sufficiency of regular troops. For many generations the sons of some families had followed father into the Dukes. But after 1945 full employment, affluence, television, motor-cars and mobility made soldier families harder to find. Promises of bedside lamps, free passes and seeing mother every Thursday failed to attract young men who had grown up in an era of softer living. Most accepted National Service duty with sardonic fatalism – 'Just our bleedin' luck'. But few were prepared to commit themselves to a regular engagement.

Because the National Servicemen were better educated, easier to teach, more apt to reason and more disposed to argue than their forebears training them for war posed some problems. In the bad old days it was no uncommon thing to consign to the infantry all those officers and men for whom no 'better' employment could be found. 'You don't need anything special for the infantry', 'Anybody can be made an infantryman' were two of the typical phrases bandied about even as late as 1940. But many changes were wrought during the Second World War, and by 1945 condescension had been superseded by admiring public regard for the battle-field's 'skilled and essential maid of all work'. Changes in methods of training necessarily preceded this change in attitude. Under the old system the aim was to automate the soldier's brain and develop reflexes enabling him to withstand the thunder and lightning of battle. Modern methods of training still had to prepare him for the shock of battle, but they now had also to inculcate the ability and desire to act spontaneously as a reasoning individual. In the new Elizabethan age Britain's young men were disinclined to accept the crude processes by which their less sophisticated predecessors had been prepared for military operations; they expected more from their superiors. And this put a premium on leadership.

Most of the men, drafted to the battalion hailed from the Dukes' traditional recruiting areas in Yorkshire, and many had relatives who had served with the regiment in the two world wars. Yorkshiremen are inclined to be taciturn, except perhaps when it comes to sport – and the capabilities of Leeds United in particular. But they are the quiet sloggers, from the stock which trudged through the fields of France for an appointment at Agincourt, with Wellington at Waterloo, and with Alexander at Anzio. The descendants of these bawdy, cheerful characters came to Minden and Pontefract fresh faced alert, keen and innocent. But they were soon to show that they lacked neither the courage, the skill, nor the humour of their forebears. For them the Korean war was an unwelcome event, but they accepted it as their destiny. For some it was to be grudgingly acknowledged as the happiest time of their lives, a welcome and unforgotten change from dreary occupations and an opportunity to see something of life and the world. But that was to be much later. At the time a memory of their gloomy buoyancy is contained in a remark made by one man as he marched to the station: 'Just my luck my name beginning with "L": it'll be down at the bottom of t'war memorial with all the dogs cocking their legs on it.'

Many of the recruits, fresh from their basic training in barrack square perfection, were a trifle uneasy when they dumped their kit bag on the station platform and reported to an NCO who brusquely ordered them to 'Look sharp' and 'move yer bodies'. But a fighting unit is the greatest of all fraternities, and feelings of trepidation were soon dispelled. Ramsay Bunbury made a habit of seeing all drafts as soon as they arrived, shaking every man's hand, asking him one or two personal questions: where he lived, where he trained and if he knew anyone in the battalion. Then he would address the group as a whole, welcoming the newcomers to the regiment, telling them that everyone in the regiment was proud of its record, that he was confident they would help to maintain and even enhance it, and finally, that every one of them was to consider himself a fully fledged member of the regimental family from that moment on.

Throughout the preparative period no one could complain of being bored. Boredom stems from inactivity or uninspired useless activity, and the Dukes were fully and gainfully occupied from Minden to Britannia Camp in Korea. In six months the recruits underwent an unbelievable transformation from ignorance to application, from ineptness to efficiency. In Germany much of the time was spent on the range. Being able to shoot and to march are two of the pragmatic age-old prerequisites of good fighting foot-soldiers, and they were qualities strongly advocated by Bunbury. Not only was he an enthusiastic shot himself, who enjoyed nothing better than a day on the range, the Dukes were almost as renowned for their proficiency in army shooting competitions as for their prowess on the rugby field. Because it would be vital to capitalize on the accuracy of small arms fire in Korea, weapon training was given top priority in the training programme.

For teaching his men to handle their weapons Bunbury's most valuable asset was the nucleus of sergeants and corporals remaining when the 're-sorting' process was completed. These were the 'old soldiers' – young in years but old in experience – who could show the young ones how to behave and how to make the best of their conditions. (It is perhaps unfortunate that the phrase 'old soldier' so often connotes individuals who never die but only fade away, and who need more supervision than a pack of monkeys.) Individually these old hands varied, but most of them knew something about the improved methods of instructing civilian soldiers. A few of them also possessed the specialized military knowledge that is the most important non-physical shortage in less professional armies than that of Britain. On the range this is vital because, despite its simplicity, shooting – like the use of complex signal equipment – is one subject which requires specialized knowledge.

In April, while the battalion's four rifle companies took ten-day turns on the ranges at Sennelager, the machine-gun platoon trained and practised on a lonely stretch of the Baltic coast set aside as a NATO field firing area. Captain Sam Robertson was a tolerant and patient platoon commander. Of medium build he had strong, rather classically moulded features with a broad rounded face, which at work wore the enigmatic expression often acquired by the professional soldier during parade hours, but in conversation lit with a pleasing warmth. Merely the fact that he was a leading member of the battalion's boxing team would have been sufficient to inspire respect. It was, in fact, his good nature and concern for their welfare that appealed to his troops. Like his commanding officer, Robertson was a shooting fetishist – but dedicated to his Vickers guns as well as being a member of the Army Shooting Eight. Teaching men the intricacies of indirect and 'barrage' machine-gun concentration needs patience, hard unremitting effort, and endurance. Under Robertson's hand the reorganized platoon began to shape up.

At this time the Dukes were not the only troops exercising on the machine-gun range, although they probably gained more from their fortnight there than some of the other units. Because this was a NATO range it happened that feeding arrangements were an American responsibility. To British troops what was offered à l'Americaine in the communal mess was attractively different if not of a higher standard than that to which they were accustomed. Unfortunately, the Dukes had barely unpacked their kit before the American and Canadian contingents who were there for practice had decided that the food was not to their liking. The combined North American protest took the form of a sit-down strike outside the dining hall. Hungry, confronted with a difference not of their making and alien to their habits, the Dukes' machine-gunners were at a loss. Reporting to Robertson, the senior corporal asked what the Dukes should do. 'Get in there and scoff the lot,' Robertson commanded. 'Never', said one of his men afterwards, 'did we enjoy such grub.'

Back in Minden the atmosphere was very much 'Rhine Army'. Like other units the Dukes had their quota of whitewash and red ochre, drill, quarter guards, and the other components of what is cynically referred to as 'Army bull'. Criticism is sometimes levelled at such 'bull' as though it were a military anachronism. Because there is a world of difference between 'bull' as a term of abuse and a clean presentable appearance, it is unfortunate that 'bull' and 'spit and polish' have become synonymous with an unbending and reactionary type of military mind. The latter, quite rightly, is to be deplored in a service where active open minds are essential. Anti-bull champions argue that Wingate's Chindits, the Israelis, the Australians and even the Royal Navy's submarine service at sea have got results without worrying too much about appearances. Nevertheless it is true to say that a man's outward appearance tends to reflect the edge of his character, just as the turn-out of a British regiment usually reflects its character also. In the British army the good soldier always dresses and acts the part.

'Toughening up' exercises and route marches, interspersed with inoculations and packing, added more than a spice of variety to the weapon training programme. There was little time for brooding about the future, the validity of lurid, oral pictures of the disagreeableness of war or the delights of Leeds or Bradford on a Saturday night. Until the pace slackened towards the end of July, the men were too tired to think of anything but bed at the end of the day. Initially the route marches were not too strenuous – little more than seven or eight miles in all. But they were enough to raise blisters on the soles of the newcomers' feet. They were healed by that universal military remedy, gentian blue, a panacea for innumerable ills in humans and animals.

'Free-for-all' exercises were more strenuous though generally more enjoyable, and in the rugged hills of Westphalia they were designed to give full scope to the ingenuity of the participants. Platoons and companies were pitted against each other, and within the bounds of realism each side was free to use its cunning, completely unhampered by restrictions limiting freedom of action. All the equipment for three days was carried, and the capacity for self-preservation of young conscripts was ably demonstrated on one occasion when a party of 'enemy' was surprised milking cows into enamel mugs in the cold light of a drizzly dawn. Chief exponent and enthusiast for these exercises was the youngest of the rifle company commanders. Thirty-two-year-old Edward Emett was a bachelor, and still a captain although he was holding a major's appointment. Never depressed, Emett had a good brain, an extravagantly realistic outlook on life – which he believed should be enjoyed to the full – a quick sharp wit and considerable military talent. He was not a typical product of the spartan regime of Wellington and the robust environment of Sandhurst. But his general air of comfortable dignity and a penchant for the fleshpots had gained him the nickname 'Baron' – a title which he endeavoured to justify by his demeanour. In the 'free-for-alls' his invention concocted many imaginative situations.

No doubt some tactical lessons were learned in the course of the field training. But the accent was on shooting and toughness. Colonel Bunbury had no illusions about the war in Korea being fought under Marquess of Queensberry rules and he was not prepared to waste time on subjects irrelevant to 'valour and suffrance'. So there were no mass callisthenics, no periods allowed to subjects such as unarmed combat. Fitness, he believed, would come through training to fight, and those sports which the Dukes tended to push *jusqu'au fanatisme* would substitute for the flexing of muscles in unison, while providing relaxation and amusement at the same time.

Towards the end of July the training grind was called to a halt. Equipment had been packed and it was time to move. A good-bye dance and a farewell cocktail party concluding with a masterly rendering of Tchaikowsky's '1812' by the regimental band and a bonfire closed the Minden chapter. Next morning, 7 August, three special trains chuffed out towards the Hook of Holland carrying 600 men of the Dukes on the first leg of their journey towards another, more sinister Hook.

2

FIGHTING FRONT

Look not back.

ROBERT BRIDGES

'That', said the Australian, pointing to a bare crescent-shaped ridge among the profusion of hills 1200 yards away, 'is the bloody Hook'. The speaker was standing on the crest of another hill capped by a single sad-looking tree. Between him and the feature whose history and limitations he went on to describe in lavish and lurid language ran the desolate valley of Sami-Chon river. His audience were 'Dukes', men from one of the platoons relieving the 3rd Royal Australian Regiment in the Commonwealth Divisional sector of the Korean front line.

This was to be their first stint in the front line since arriving in the Land of the Morning Calm. As they plodded up the steep paths to the trenches and dug-outs vacated by the mature and confident Australians, many of the young Yorkshiremen felt a positive sense of relief. They had been trained to the last hair – or thought they had; they had been brought into the arena; and now they wanted to get on with the fight, get it over and get back home. Nearly all of them had yet to hear the dull thud of an enemy field gun or the hollow pop of a mortar, the whine of an approaching shell, and the roar which preceded the crash of its burst. Only the older officers and NCOs had seen action before and they certainly did not relish the idea of being bombed, or mortared, or shelled, or sniped again. But their fears were obscured by that air of cool, unfussy efficiency which the British expect from professional soldiers. Whether they had seen battle or not, what they were most frightened of was not fear of wounds or death, but fear of being afraid.

In fact the battalion was being broken in gently. Except as an occasional target for shells and mortar bombs, or the erratic attention of a Chinese sniper, the hill which the Dukes were now occupying had seen no sign of the enemy for the past ten months. Yong Dong was notorious, but not as the locale of recurrent battles. Indeed its popularity derived from the relatively placid atmosphere of the place, and a constant stream of visitors came for the view. From Yong Dong it was possible to look up and down the Commonwealth front, out beyond the British zone of responsibility in the United Nations Main Line of Resistance. From the north of the Imjin to a point on the east coast twenty-five miles north of the 38th Parallel, the MLR snaked across Korea. In the American sectors it was marked by a long bunkered trench system with an occasional secondary line. Beyond the trenches lay No Man's Land; beyond No Man's Land were the Chinese. For the most part these trenches ran up hill and down dale irrespective of tactical considerations. The Americans favoured a clear-cut delineation of responsibility – a line beyond which the enemy operated and behind which the tempo of war decreased in direct proportion to the distance behind the front. Fighting other than in the forward areas was to be deplored; to them the very idea of Chinese parties infiltrating and operating behind the U.N. lines was wholly abhorrent.

But in the area of the Commonwealth sector a continuous line of trenches would not have halted the Chinese. According to Chairman Mao 'ground is the handmaid of victory', and the Chinese had quickly learned to turn the inhospitable hills and desolate valleys of Korea to good advantage. The only sure way of stopping them breaking through was to select features of tactical importance and to hold these at all costs. In the British sector the Hook was one such feature; another in the neighbouring American sector was called 'Betty Grable' because its scenic shapeliness was vaguely reminiscent of the film lovely of that name. Hills like these were the scenes of the kind of bitter fighting which men of an older generation will associate with Cassino. Yong Dong was not among them.

Yet Yong Dong was also counted among the hills dubbed 'vital ground'. Its importance as a key position was never tested only because Chinese tactics were dictated by the terrain. Capturing the Hook would have been a necessary preliminary to the assault of Yong Dong, and the wide open valley of the Sami-Chon would have been an ideal killing ground. In short, Yong Dong was an excellent training ground for a fresh unit – an area where men could make mistakes and not have to pay for them; where young soldiers could learn the difference between incoming and outgoing shells, and where old soldiers could forget how they had chased Rommel across Africa or the Japanese out of Burma and learn the arts of static war; where stealth and cunning which would match that of the Chinese could be acquired, and the steel nerves needed on patrol could be developed; where, above all, patience could be developed and practised – patience to enable men to live on the same hill for months on end, waiting for an attack which would probably never come, yet remain ready for it at any moment of the night and day.

Some of the Dukes were already familiar with Yong Dong. As indefatigable Egyptian gulli-gulli men went through their traditional routine aboard the troopship *Orwell* at Port Said, men of the Welch Regiment were already teaching the operational routine on Yong Dong to the Dukes' advance party. The machine-gunner, Sam Robertson, found himself in charge. Major Walter Skelsey, Ramsay Bunbury's second-in-command had brought the advance party to Pusan. But from there he had flown on to Kure, taking Captain Bernard Kilner the transport officer with him. Walter Skelsey, due soon to swap the role of second-in-command for that of staff officer, was a hardworking and likeable man. Chubby, red-faced, quietly friendly, Skelsey was not a specially exciting figure. Like one of Somerset Maugham's colonial commissioners, he was loyal, understanding and wholly trustworthy. But in the shadow of Ramsay Bunbury his character was uninspiring.

In Germany Bunbury had learned that battalions arriving in Korea were tested and judged on their performance in a diabolical set-piece exercise before they were committed to battle. Moreover opinion on how it performed in this series of make-believe situations appeared to dog a battalion throughout its tour in Korea. A poor showing tended to reflect on everybody from the commanding officer down to the last-joined private soldier – especially on the commanding officer. With the regiment's honour as well as his own reputation at stake Bunbury was determined to do well and Skelsey was told that if he did nothing else he should try to discover the problems and pitfalls of the exercise. Bunbury was not disappointed and when he arrived in Korea, having left the *Orwell* in Singapore and flown up to Seoul, Skelsey quietly handed him a copy of the problems and their solutions. Possession of this information did not automatically guarantee a good showing, but careful stage-management went a long way towards it.

From November to March winter envelops Korea, with freezing cold winds from Siberia howling in. At night the temperature drops to well below zero and the inexperienced newcomers to the country had much to learn about the tactics of survival in arctic conditions. Fortunately this winter of 1952–53 was relatively mild – clear and sharp at night, with a warm and cheering sun almost every day. Fortunately also the British Government was now providing proper winter clothing for its men in Korea. Heavy woollen socks, the long white pants which are familiarly known as 'Long Johns', crocheted string vests and heavy fleece trousers were issued for inner protection. Over these went gaberdine trousers, a thick flannel shirt and heavy pullover. Completing the ensemble a combat jacket, topped by a fleecy-lined and hooded parka, created the appearance of an overgrown penguin. Heavy leather ski-boots with metal toe-caps and thick woollen mittens covered by three-digited gloves – one for the thumb, one for the trigger finger, and one for the rest – protected hands and feet.

Provided the individual knew how to wear it, this clothing was adequate. Nobody got frostbite and there was very little trench foot. Lying out on patrol, however, the Dukes found that the cold still managed to penetrate to the marrow of their bones and they experimented with pocket warmers, resembling large cigarette lighters. Filled with spirit and lit by a glowing asbestos wick these miniature radiators could burn for 24 hours. Twelve of them distributed about the vital parts of the body – at the knees, in the crutch, and in the small of the back – helped to alleviate the misery – except for the feet, and all that could be done to keep them warm was to wriggle the toes.

In the line – at Yong Dong, the Hook or elsewhere – men lived in their slit trenches, bunkers and dug-outs. The latter were known by the British as 'hoochies', and by the Australians as 'wacks'. Dangerous contraptions, varying from the efficient but smelly to the highly explosive, were used to warm these shelters. By far the most common type was the petrol 'chuffer', but all the so-called space-heaters worked on similar lines – burning either petrol or diesel in a round metal stove. Theoretically, the flow of fuel from a can outside the bunker controlled the temperature in the 'hoochi'. But chuffers were temperamental and trick machines requiring delicate handling, and one man in every 'hoochi' was designated chuffer mechanic. Many considered his appointment should have carried danger money. The stoves had two temperatures: stone cold and red hot, and coaxing them from cold to roasting was the devil's work. Yet they would occasionally flare up for no apparent reason, and during November and December 1952, the Dukes suffered more casualties from space-heater burns than from enemy action.

An earlier generation would have found the physical condition, the improvizations and the type of operations at Yong Dong in November, 1952, not dissimilar from those of the Western Front during the winter of 1916. The only difference was that in the First World War, as in the Second, the troops could usually look forward to reasonably good conditions in a recognized form of accommodation out of the line. Not so in Korea, except for short and infrequent leaves to Japan or when one's time came to go home. Undamaged houses were rare and generally infested with rats and lice.

Because of a rigid insistence on keeping clothes and bodies clean lice were not usually a problem. But rats were. Rats, akin to the allegorical pests 'with bowler hats and spats' which were reputed to inhabit the mythical QM store of 1940, lived and thrived in all the dug-outs. Like humans, rats feel the cold and seek warmth, especially where food is to be had. In the forward areas the timbered roofs and sand-bagged walls of the 'hoochies' provided them with admirable nesting places. Safely ensconced they would watch for a scrap of food to be left about before descending with rare impudence to eat it. There was little sense trying to kill these sleek monsters. Not only were they adept at dodging missiles or a quick lunge with a bayonet; if poisoned they returned to their nests to die, and the smell of their rotting bodies usually meant the removal of six feet of earth cover and the complete reconstruction of the bunker. Traps were the only means of catching them, and it was almost impossible to buy traps in Korea.

In the course of time some men came to accept that living cheek by jowl with rats was a fact of life, and familiar characters were given names like Pinky and Perky. Others, men like Baron Emett, never overcame their feelings of revulsion and constantly campaigned to reduce their numbers and antics. One unfortunate individual had a nervous break-down following a particularly revolting experience. Sleeping with his mouth half-open, he had instinctively and involuntarily closed his jaws on the head of an inquisitive rat peering down his gullet. Emett himself had had a rat scamper across his face, and thereafter he could sleep only when he knew his slumber would be rat-free. In practical terms this meant sleeping on the table in his command post bunker, where the duty orderly or a signaller could watch for rodent sorties.

In the early days, before he came to terms with the rats, Robertson tried pot shots at them with his revolver. But he ran short of ammunition. Having fired his quota of twelve rounds of ·38 ammunition (without killing any rats), he had to ask the Quartermaster, Lieutenant Albert Parr, for another twelve rounds. 'Where', queried the Quartermaster, 'are twelve dead Chinamen?' He then went on to explain that there was no reserve pistol ammunition in Korea; pistols were an outmoded weapon in the kind of fighting experienced so far, and no one had reckoned on their use as rat exterminators. (In the dug-outs men slept on their ground-sheets; any form of improvised bed was a rare luxury. But one officer, with commendable foresight, had provided himself with an air mattress. When it developed a puncture he indented for a repair kit. A few days later the voice of a CQMS was heard over the radio: 'Who', he demanded incredulously, 'is riding a bicycle up there?')

Rats aside, Robertson had been fully occupied with his beloved Vickers guns ever since his arrival. The open countryside was ideal for the weapon which had first established its real worth in the Russo–Japanese War. And from Yong Dong even the approaches to the Hook could be swept with a hail of bullets; from positions flanking Yong Dong it was possible to enshroud the front-line trenches with a steel curtain of ·303 bullets. But organization of a machine-gun barrage requires a good deal of pre-arrangement, and not everybody shared Robertson's enthusiasm. Rifle company commanders had been bequeathed a couple of American Browning machine guns by the previous occupants of their positions. In these guns they saw a hefty reserve of firepower under their own hand, and Robertson had to convince each of them that the guns would be put to better use if he welded their tasks into a fire plan based on his own Vickers.

Persuading others that his plan was best for everybody concerned was sometimes even more difficult. Indirect machine-gun fire should fit into the artillery fire-plan, to cover ground unswept by shell fire. The ground has to be surveyed, air photographs studied, gun positions reconnoitred and set up, and tasks have to be worked out for each gun in detail. Water for cooling the guns has to be provided and ammunition carted up to the gun positions. Aiming marks also have to be provided for both day and night shooting. In Korea the steep gradients of the hills ruled out the use of conventional aiming posts, and a system depending on mirrors was devised. Combined with the draping of blankets across the aperture of the machine-gun firing positions to preserve the warmth and conceal the light, a conventional soldier who was not au fait with Robertson's methods may be forgiven for expressing surprise. Stepping into one of the Dukes' machine-gun posts during an action gave the impression of entering a cacophonous Stygian pit. The gunners, firing on fixed lines, had no need to look outside; their sights were set on mirror images and their whole concentration centred on the smooth passage of belts of ammunition through the breech block.

At this time the Black Watch were occupying the Hook, and their Commanding Officer, David Rose, whose lean military good looks would have fitted nicely into one of Sapper's novels, was not a machine gun enthusiast. Nor did he care much for his supporting weapons being coordinated into a plan which might reduce their worth to him. In the tradition of Scotch regiments the élan associated with men using cold steel had more appeal than specialists at overhead fire, and he testily told

Robertson that his machine-gunners 'would be better off with bayonets'.

On Yong Dong the bayonet saw more use as a tin opener than as an appendage to the muzzle of a rifle. No enemy were to be seen; by day the Chinese were cleaning and oiling their weapons, or eating cabbage soup in bunkers carved into the rear slopes of the hills facing the Dukes' positions. Nothing moved on the forward slopes, nothing stirred in the frozen paddy fields of the Sami-Chon valley. The only reminder of the existence of an active and dangerous war was the drumming of friendly artillery. But Chinese sentries in camouflaged pits were watching and waiting for an opportunity to show their teeth.

After a month on 'the Dong' the Dukes were considered ready for more active duty. They had learned something of the art of working by night and resting by day; they had discovered the real value of sleep; they had become accustomed to being woken at every conceivable hour of the day and night, and they had learned to relax – the secret of being able to sit down and crumple up like an old sock in a sleep from which they could jerk themselves into a hundred per cent alertness in a second. They had learned to live in tiny, sack-lined bunkers in close proximity to four other men and to overlook their companions' annoying and sometimes revolting habits. They had learned that keeping warm necessitated a special hard discipline – insulated boots were of little use if socks weren't changed often enough or spare socks weren't kept dry. They had learned that throwing a match was not the best way of seeing whether petrol was running. They had discovered that modern rifles, Brens, and Stens had the same qualities as the old Martini, of which Kipling wrote:

Don't treat your Martini as a cross-eyed old bitch.
She's human as you are and treat her as such.
And she'll fight for the young British soldier.

They had come to realize that their safety lay in their own hands, that if they dozed while on sentry duty or fell asleep while on patrol they might never wake again. Accidents with loaded weapons had taught them that firearms in careless hands cannot distinguish between friend and foe. They had learned to make themselves as comfortable as conditions would allow, to make improvisations that would give them more room in the squalid bunkers, to keep their trenches clean, and their latrines hygienic. Above all they had learned to work as a team.

On 1 December, the Dukes were ordered to relieve the Durham Light Infantry in a sector of the line a few miles farther north. A French Canadian battalion took over 'the Dong' and, as the relieving troops struggled with their kit in the communication trenches, the Chinese artillery opened fire. The first few shells crashed down around the positions occupied by one of the platoons of B company and a second salvo straddled the company headquarters command post. Nobody was hurt but the explosions provided a salutary lesson. Four weeks in relatively close proximity to a rarely visible and seemingly tranquil enemy had blunted the earlier feelings of apprehension. This was a reminder that the Chinese had teeth which they were prepared to use when an opportunity was presented. A touch of macabre humour was provided by one man obeying a last-minute call of nature. In demonstrating that a man can run with his trousers down a certain saying sometimes attributed to Confucius was disproved.

An abrupt change in the weather coincided with the move. Roads and tracks froze, and as Chinese activity flared up the war suddenly seemed more real. Any movement which could be seen from the Chinese side precipitated a storm of shells and mortar bombs, and the Dukes suffered their first casualties from enemy action. Before the month was out two men had been killed and eight wounded.

Behind the hills life continued at a more or less normal pace, undisturbed by anything more than the harassment of an occasional bombardment. By day men could sit about in the wintry sun, sheltered from the cold north-westerly wind by the hills they were defending. Outside Ramsay Bunbury's command post bunker, below the crest of a hill in the centre of the new position, a roughly hewn terrace provided the facilities of an orderly room. Here, on milder days, justice would be dispensed to malefactors. Arrowed notices and a galaxy of dazzling sign-boards indicated the whereabouts of the various bunkers, the Regimental Aid Post, and the Signals and Intelligence sections; at the foot of the hill RSM Pearce presided over a covey of jeeps and regimental police, close by two essential erections of tarpaulins and wood. One of these was the battalion cookhouse, supervised by Sergeant Fielden, the other a bathhouse super-vised by a smoke-blackened Korean. Behind the hill the adminis-trative essentials seemed somewhat remote from the war. But life on the forward slopes of the hill had few reminders of peace-time routine. In daylight, movement outside the trenches and dug-outs quickly prompted Chinese reaction. Within a matter of seconds shells would be thundering down or the sharp crack of a sniper's bullet would demonstrate that the sullen hillsides opposite were still occupied by an alert and observant enemy.

Inability to move by day inevitably meant compressing any-thing that had to be done into the hours of darkness. And there was always plenty to be done – trenches to be dug, wire to be laid, dug-outs to be improved, rations and other essential stores ferried up to the forward positions. No defences are ever perfect, and the rifle companies had an insatiable appetite for wire, pickets and timber.

Some locations were more vulnerable than others. In the area initially occupied by Emett's 'D' company three-quarters of a mile of so-called goat-track led to the forward positions. In reality this track was a trench about two feet wide and four to six feet deep, and it was evident that part of it was under Chin-ese observation. So also was a rough track which traversed the front of Emett's positions. One stretch of this trench, known as the 'Two hundred yards dash' was well known to the Chinamen, and although jeeps could use it in the dark anyone who tried to do so in daylight was taking a suicidal risk, which Ramsey Bunbury decreed was unjustified in normal circumstances.

Yet men did take this risk, and sometimes they paid for it. One who paid was the Signal officer, Lieutenant Reddington. Tall, slim and good looking, with a rather long face and straight features John Reddington had the smooth youthful appearance of a schoolboy. Rather highly strung – with a character that was both strong and gentle – the rougher side of life had not yet pared all the illusions of life from his outlook. Five minutes on the 'Two hundred yards dash' were to effect a rapid change. On this particular day Reddington had gone up to the front line to bring back one of his signallers. For some reason which must have seemed very trivial after the event it was important for him to get back to battalion headquarters. En route, just before the start of the critical part of the track, he stopped at the mortar platoon's command post. 'What do you think', he asked Lieutenant Bill Blakey, the mortar officer, 'Shall I risk it?' Blakey, an impulsive character, had seen others get through. 'Go on', he replied, 'Make a dash for it.' So Reddington's driver set off. But he had failed to engage the jeep's four-wheel drive, and half way along the 'two hundred yards dash' the engine faltered and stalled. Simultaneously shells screamed over and the vehicle was engulfed in smoke. Reddington's companions were only shaken, but a splinter of steel had struck their luckless officer. In trying to save minutes, Reddington had forfeited an eye and a military career.

By the middle of December it began to look as if the Chinese were conscious of the approach of Christmas, and did not propose to spend it hibernating in their bunkers waiting for a break in the recessed armistice negotiations. The eerie waste between the U.N. and Chinese lines became a psychological as well as an infantry battle ground, and the Dukes busied themselves trying to catch the unseen and rarely detected 'Christmas card' patrols which dumped propaganda leaflets in front of their positions at night. Meantime Chinese loudspeakers blared across No Man's Land, broadcasting sinister advice and pop music. Unmoved by diatribes concerning their being used as tools of Uncle Sam, the British troops could listen to the tunes of the Jazz Age of the roaring twenties, and write home enclosing the Christmas card souvenirs they had picked up on patrol. 'Where there is peace there is blessing', said one on the outside. 'Do not fight for the Americans any longer' was the message on the inside 'unless you want to die.' Fortunately only one man of the Dukes did die about this time, and he was mortally wounded by one of the mortar bombs which alternated with the Chinese plea for that precious Communist commodity, peace.

3

THE BLOODY HOOK

Now's the day, and now's the hour.
See the front o' battle lour.

ROBERT BURNS,
Scots Wha Hae wi' Wallace Bled.

In calling it 'bloody' those who knew the ridge labelled Hook used an appropriate adjective. Much blood had stained the ground around the four main hummocks of this crescent-shaped hog's back. In March, 1952, when it was occupied by Canada's 'Princess Pats', a savage assault had cost the Chinese at least thirty-one dead. Considering the Princess Patricia's had fought a hand to hand engagement for more than two hours, Canadian casualties were surprisingly light – four killed and ten wounded. But this action was only the forerunner of others which would exact a far heavier toll.

For the next eight months an uneasy calm settled over the Hook, disturbed only by bombardments which grew steadily more intense as Chinese artillery techniques improved. Activity flared up on other sectors of the U.N. front, but most of the Chinese effort was concentrated on building up and strengthening their own defences. By the late autumn of 1952 these stretched back for some twenty miles, and it was estimated that they had 900 pieces of artillery and seven Chinese armies totalling 160,000 men facing the U.N. Armies. Against the background of the truce talks at Panmunjon the American Far East

Intelligence experts predicted that the Communists would be content to sit in their trenches and wait for the U.N. to make concessions to end the war. At that time a major Chinese offensive seemed out of the question. And, in fact, no major offensive did develop. Nevertheless fighting flared up in October when the Chinese attempted to seize key points on the ancient northern invasion route to Seoul.

The Hook was one such key position. Here, where the U.N. Main Line of Resistance turned sharply south-west, away from the natural line of the Sami-Chon valley, 'the Hook' was a tactical hinge. The central ridge inside the 100-metre contour which gave this precariously held piece of real estate its name was only 120 metres above sea level. On the right it was connected to another ridge known as 'Sausage' and on the left rear to 'Pt 121'. As both Sausage and Pt 121 were set back from the Hook proper, they were less vulnerable. Moreover in front of both these features the ground fell sharply away, while three ridges, Warsaw, Green Finger and Seattle converged on the Hook. Another knife-edge ridge, known as Long Finger ran up to the Sausage area, but this was dominated by both Sausage and the Hook. For the Chinese the easiest approach to the Hook from their main position on 'Pheasant' was across the valley, up the far end of the Green Finger ridge, and along its broad crest. Less negotiable approaches could be made along Warsaw or along Ronson from Seattle. The importance of the Hook stemmed from the fact that it dominated the Sami-chon valley. From the Hook two vital crossings of the Imjin carrying the U.N. lines of communication to the eastern sector could be observed. Beyond the Sami-chon valley lay the flat countryside of the Imjin valley and the road to the South Korean capital. In short a breakthrough at the Hook made possible the systematic roll-up of virtually the whole west sector of the American Eighth Army Front; and, as the hills five to ten miles south of the Imjin provided the only suitable ground for establishing another U.N. defence line, to fall back would have been disastrous.

In October a decision was taken to adjust responsibilities in the front line. The effect of this decision was to cause the Commonwealth Division to sidestep to the left, giving up three thousand yards on the extreme right of their sector to the South Korean 1st R.O.K. Division, and taking over an equivalent portion of the line on the left. The sector on the left included the Hook, then held by the 7th U.S. Marines and on 27 October the 1st Battalion The Black Watch was ordered to take over from them. Meantime it appears that the Chinese had also decided on some readjustments and on the night of 26 October they started to shell the Marines' positions on the Hook. Until this bombardment actually started the extent to which the Chinese had developed their artillery techniques had not been apparent. But it was soon evident that not only was their fire more accurate but it was also far more concentrated than ever before. The effect on the Hook was devastating.

As fighting men the U.S. Marines have shown themselves second to none. They have established a reputation for being tough, daring and resourceful. But the spade, that universal and important weapon which has averted many defeats and saved many lives, is no more popular with the Marines than it is with other soldiers. A single shallow convoluted rifleman's trench ran round the face of the Hook and linked it with Sausage. Sandbagged and fire slotted bunkers had been built into this trench system at thirty-yard intervals. As many of the entrances faced directly towards the Chinese lines of approach they afforded only limited protection. Because digging in the stony ground was hard and heavy work the Marines had done little to improve the defences. For the sweat they saved they were to pay dearly in blood.

Like nearly all Chinese attacks on U.N. positions, the assault on the 7th Marines followed an established pattern known as the 'one point – two sides method'. The essence of it was fixing the objective as the base of a V, and then enveloping it with a two-pronged sweep round the sides. The attacks were characterized by their intensity – a quality the Chinese described as 'three fierce actions – fierce fires, fierce assaults, fierce follow-up'. Once an objective had been decided upon the tactics were routine. First the 'fierce fires' by way of a ferocious bombardment, then the frontal attack to engage the defenders and draw fire, so revealing the extent of the defences, and finally the envelopment by the followers-up on the flanks.

On this occasion the Chinese barrage had not lifted before the first of the attacking Chinese infantry charged up to the Hook defences. The Marines, dazed and deafened by the pounding they had sustained, opened up with everything they had and the carnage on the narrow ridge known as Green Finger was ghastly. But the impetus of the rush carried the Chinese forward over their own dead and dying. Momentarily they were checked by the remnants of the barbed wire which had screened the Marines' positions. But great gaps had been torn in the wire by the shells, and the olive green waves swept through to the shallow trenches. 'They looked like devils running through hell', a Marine corporal said later. 'All they needed were pitchforks.'

With the Marines on the Hook fully engaged, phase two of the Chinese assault now began to develop. Up from the re-entrants below the Ronson and Warsaw ridges flanking the Hook fresh tides of Chinese infantry swept in to complete the envelopment and clear the adjoining ridges of Sausage and Pt 121. Desperate hand-to-hand fighting raged as the Chinese steadily exploited their tenuous foothold on the American position. The Marines resisted stubbornly, yielding ground yard by yard and taking a heavy toll of the Chinese. Behind the Hook and on the flanking hills, across the long neglected paddy fields, high-pitched screams of pain, fury and frustration could clearly be heard above the cacophony of bursting shells, exploding grenades and rattle of automatic weapons. Believing that a break-through was imminent the Turkish commander of the defences in the next locality ordered his troops to be ready to 'bug out' if the Chinese broke through.

Colonel Mike Delaney, Commanding Officer of the 7th Marines, had no intention of letting the Chinese break through. It had been his proud boast that the 7th Marines 'held' the Hook, and because he was supposed to be handing it over to 'a British outfit' that very day, Delaney considered national as well as Marine honour was at stake. Supported by one of the biggest artillery concentrations of the Korean War to date and preceded by a heavy air strike, a counter-attack was launched.

Shortly after noon a Harvard spotter plane, slow-moving in relation to the aircraft which were to follow, flew up the U.N. line and circled the Hook. Puffs of anti-aircraft fire from hitherto unsuspected guns dug into the the hills on the other side of No Man's Land pursued the Harvard as its pilot swung round and over their line. Over the radio the pilot was describing in airman's language the targets selected for the incoming fighter-bombers. Then the first V-flock formation whined in, turning to peel off singly to rocket the slopes and the positions so recently seized from Delaney's Marines. As one lot of planes pulled out of their dives, rolling and corkscrewing away – back to the airfields near Seoul or the carriers in the China sea – another formation took their place. Some carried rockets, others dropped napalm bombs.

A shattering, gritty roar denoted the rocket; a muffled thump and an amber and black ball of flame signified the release of a napalm bomb. Distance robs the latter of its visual impact. A mile or more away the effect of a scorching eruption of jellied petrol and the frenzied sizzle of burning vegetation is lost. But close to the scene of a strike the vile globules of consuming flame present a truly terrifying spectacle.

After the air strike it was the turn of the artillery again, and the din rose to another monstrous crescendo. The whole hillside rocked as the Marines moved up to counterattack and retake the positions in which many of their 'buddies' had perished. At a cost of two hundred casualties they eventually succeeded. Next morning Delaney congratulated his company commanders and announced for the benefit of the record that the Hook was the property of the 7th Marines and 'no other sonofabitch would say different'.

Delaney's experiences and the swaying fortunes of the 7th Marines did not seem to augur well for the Black Watch. Knowing that his Jocks would be replacing the Marines as soon as the situation was stabilized, Lieutenant-Colonel David Rose had watched with special concern. 'I'm giving you the Hook, David, and I know you'll hold it,' his brigadier had said. In more direct terms what he meant was that the Black Watch would stay on the Hook come hell or high water.

Brigadier Joe Kendrew was a likeable, athletically built man – he had been a fine rugby footballer in his day – with the character and outlook of a true professional soldier.[1] In peacetime his interests focused on robust sporting activities, but in war all the vigour of the rugby field was directed to soldiering. In his mind the problems of rugby and war were probably not dissimilar. Successful performance in either demanded concentration on the objective, team spirit and all-out determination. He might use sporting analogies and express himself in casual terms, but there was nothing casual about Joe Kendrew's intentions. If he said he expected David Rose to hold the Hook, it would be held, or the Black Watch would need a new commanding officer.

Two years younger than his brigadier, David Rose was not Kendrew's favourite C.O. Rose had shown his mettle and proved his worth in four campaigns. But he had all the clannishness, independence of character and boundless self-confidence of the traditional Highland soldier. To one outside the family of the 1st Battalion The Black Watch the inconsequential air and unruffled calm which befitted this handsome Scot could suggest a casual approach to the business of war in Korea. With the family it was different. Whether they were true Scots or hailed

[1] Later Major-General Sir Douglas Kendrew, Governor of Western Australia. He was captain of the England Fifteen in 1935, and already had three DSOs – one won in North Africa, and two in Italy. At this time he was forty-two years old.

from one of the counties represented by the other regiments of Kendrew's brigade, the Jocks of the Black Watch had an intense pride in their unit.[2]

The Black Watch was a first-class fighting regiment, and they knew it. They saw their battalion, and their regiment, as a cut above the Dukes or the Kings or the Royal Fusiliers. This tended to set them apart and to cause them to look inwards at the family of which the dashing, debonair David Rose was the head. Under his direction the regiment ran smoothly, efficiently and happily – almost casually, in fact. There was none of the fluster and flurry associated with the popular television image of short-tempered bawling commanding officers whose knowledge and ability appear to be in inverse proportion to the noise they make. Every Jock knew his job and had the confidence to fulfil it to the best of his ability. No man can do more than his best, and it is not every commander who can bring out the best in his troops. Joe Kendrew and David Rose both had this quality although their attitudes to life were very different.

As soon as he was able to get up to the Hook, David Rose set out with his rifle company commanders to reconnoitre the ground. The U.S. Marines had obviously taken about as much as they could take, and they made no secret of their anxiety to get away as speedily as possible. Delaney himself was full of gloomy forebodings: 'It's my guess these bastards will have you out of it inside twenty-four hours', he said, 'and that's stretching it a piece!' On the Hook itself little attempt had been made to reinstate the defences from the shambles created by the successive Chinese and American bombardments. In the course of the fighting 156 of the original 158 front line bunkers had been destroyed and most of them were full of bodies. On the crest and forward slopes of the hill the ground had been pulverized. Outpost positions had disappeared completely. Communication

[2] There is an apocryphal story of an argument between two Lancashire lads who found themselves in the Black Watch. It is reputed to have ended by one of them saying with crushing superiority: 'Ah've been a Jock longer than tha.'

trenches barely deep enough even in their prime had caved in and were now mere furrows, ludicrously inadequate.

Continued Chinese interest in the position was quickly demonstrated when Rose started his reconnaissance. Once over the crest, incautious movement attracted a volley of mortar bombs. Failing to take notice of this brought another volley and another . . . and then, the Chinese artillery joined in. Consequently Rose's ideas on what would have to be done when he took over had to be formulated in the prone position, in circumstances akin to a film set from *All Quiet on the Western Front*.

Back at Delaney's command post the U.S. Marine commander elaborated the difficulties facing those occupying the Hook. Because of heavy clay soil and the limestone outcrops which seemed to erupt at every tactical site, digging was damned hard work. In another month when the ground froze, it would be worse. The Chinese were very active at night – so active that the Marines had managed to sleep no more than two or three hours in twenty-four for over three weeks. In his experience, Delaney averred, Guadalcanal and Saipan were a walkover compared with the Hook. 'See any combat yourself, Dave?' he queried suddenly. Rose winced; he did not care for the easy American familiarity with which first names are used on very short acquaintance, nor did he care for 'Dave'. 'A little', he replied, 'here and there.' 'Well', said Delaney, 'you'll soon see I'm not kidding. It's a lousy place and those Chinese are tricky bastards.'

Like every other British officer in Korea, David Rose was a staunch admirer of the United States Marines. But he had seen that there were some major flaws in Delaney's defensive layout and it was clear that the 7th Marines had little zest for fieldworks and entrenchments. When the Chinese attacked the Hook the Marines had fought bravely, but at a disadvantage. Following a policy of 'live and let live' they had grown lax, and their defence of the Hook had rested on a single long trench across the front of the ridge. Once this had gone there was nothing else

– no secondary trench systems, no defence 'in depth'. But this was neither the time nor the place for a British officer to tell a United States Marine his business.

David Rose returned to Brigade Headquarters and reported on what he had seen. Joe Kendrew sympathized; this was obviously a problem for the high command. So Rose was whisked along to see Major-General M. M. A. R. West, the Commonwealth Division commander. Mike West was another big man. He had commanded an infantry brigade at Kohima, scene of the bloody battle in Burma which, with Alamein, Midway, and Stalingrad, was one of the turning points of the Second World War. Like Kendrew, he always drove his own jeep, though less ferociously, and he liked to stride around the forward positions seeing the layout himself. When he heard what David Rose had to say, a meeting with the American Corps Commander, Lieutenant-General Paul Kendall, was quickly arranged. General Kendall wasted no time in getting down to essentials. 'How do you propose to set about getting the place re-fortified?' he asked. Rose's answer was that his plan would be to take a leaf out of the Chinese book. He would dig and tunnel a whole new series of bunkers whose entrances faced away from the line of Chinese fire. So far as was possible, British style weapons pits would replace the American foxholes and be re-sited away from the old locations where the ground had been pulverized by shells. New bunkers and tunnels in the hillside would allow his Jocks to shelter and rest in comparative safety and the re-location of the fighting trenches should bring some economy of the materials used for revetting – all of which had to be carried up under shell fire. The commander of the U.S. 1st Corps agreed. 'You can have all the help you need,' he said. 'Right', said Rose. 'I'd like 800 Korean labourers and,' turning to General West, 'a troop of Sappers.'

The Black Watch moved up and officially took over the Hook on 14 November. Their appearance surprised some of the outgoing Marines. 'The way I heard it' said one black American soldier, 'only the officers was white; the enlisted guys was all coloured. Thought I might make a transfer!' Asked what things were like, the Marines said tersely, 'It's a real sonofabitch'.

The Jocks had good reason to believe that life on the Hook would continue to be a sonofabitch. As part of his plan to regain the initiative Rose had been sending patrols into No Man's Land since the beginning of November. And on 4 November one of these patrols ran into trouble directly below the Hook. Apparently from out of the blue, but more probably from the shelter of a cave they had dug into the slopes of the Warsaw ridge, some forty Chinamen suddenly materialized and fell on the Black Watch patrol. In the ensuing fracas the young officer commanding the patrol and five Jocks were killed, six other men were wounded and two were never seen again. Only three men escaped.

On the night of the 14th the Korean labourers were brought up and set to digging. By the morning they were exhausted, and it was up to the Jocks to finish the task. If they needed an incentive the evidence in the numbers of bodies they encountered in the course of their excavations was enough to convince them that it could be a case of 'dig or die'. The Marines had not dug; in consequence many of them had died. The Jocks grumbled and swore as their entrenching tools sank into the crumbly soil. But when the tempo of the shelling increased they would be glad they had been driven so hard. Meantime, as they dug, wiring parties were erecting an elaborate barbed-wire fence to shield the new defences, and the battalion signallers were laying out a complex pattern of communications which would be capable of withstanding the heaviest bombardment. Rose had observed that whenever a position was over-run, its demise was preceded by a communications black-out; wireless aerials were shot away and telephone lines cut. To obviate this his QM, Captain Nobby Clark, was ordered to procure extra wireless sets and telephones to double and treble the means by which Rose could talk to men in the forward positions no matter what happened. To get them

Clark had to wage a battle of his own and, in his own words, there were quite a few staff officers to be 'put in their place'. But he won, the radios and telephones arrived and when the work was finished every section commander could report to the Battalion Command Post.

A sufficiency of communications permitted Rose considerably greater flexibility than had been possible hitherto. While his men were fighting it out in their foxholes Colonel Delaney's demands for artillery support had been limited by safety considerations. What Rose proposed was to curtail the accepted danger limits and to hem his men in with a blazing screen. As soon as a company commander realized his positions were in danger of being overwhelmed, he was to order his men into the newly dug bunkers and tunnels. He would then signal 'Tin Hat'. This was a code word triggering an artillery Defensive Fire plan of airburst shells directly above the trenches the Jocks had just vacated. Theoretically the assault would be shattered on its objective, and when the barrage lifted the Jocks could emerge from their shelters and clear up the mess. In practice the plan worked – up to a point.

Rose had reckoned on ten days' grace before the Chinese attacked again; he got four and the new defences were only halfway to completion. After the first day the frequency of desultory shelling of the Hook, Sausage and Pt 121 had steadily increased. Moreover, as any move on the forward slopes invariably attracted a prompt salvo of mortar bombs the really vital work had to be confined to the hours of darkness. Even then the situation was still hazardous. Every now and then the screech and whirr of shells, sounding like some furious gathering of witches on Walpurgis-night, heralded another stonk. The Chinese were searching blindly for the working parties. Sometimes they succeeded and men stringing out more wire or digging weapon pits were engulfed in shrapnel. For the unlucky ones the war was over.

The Second Battle of the Hook started about 7 pm on 18

November. At dusk, two companies of Chinese infantry left their positions on Pheasant and jogged across the valley to Green Finger. Here on previous nights, they had dug a couple of caves in which 200 of them could shelter until the moment for the final assault. They reached their first objective undetected and the first indication of an impending attack came over the wireless from one of the Black Watch standing patrols on Warsaw, 500 yards below the forward positions on the Hook.

Within minutes of reporting that men could be heard moving about below, the patrol was on the air again. They had clashed with the Chinese and were surrounded. No more was heard of that patrol. Half an hour later the company deployed on the Hook was attacked from three different directions.

Other than calling down the pre-arranged artillery fire there was little that David Rose could do at this stage. The outcome of the battle now depended on the men in the forward platoons. In such a situation one of the British Army Training Manuals says, 'Junior commanders must lead. . . . Someone has to lead men in a crisis – and that is the officer's job, the job of the company and platoon commanders.' The Black Watch company and platoon commanders did everything and more than could be expected of them. In the early stages of the battle Second-Lieutenant Michael Black, cut off and under repeated attack, sent back such cheerful and reassuring reports that his company commander, Major Angus Irwin, was constrained to ask him on the wireless if he was really as happy as he sounded. 'Are you happy where you are?' he queried. 'No, never have been', replied Black. 'Don't be a clown,' retorted Irwin. 'Out.'

Later, Lieutenant John Moncrieff, the Battalion Intelligence officer, intercepted another conversation:

Black: Our own DF is falling short. Can you rectify this?

Irwin: It is not our DF.

Black: Then some enemy are throwing grenades at us.

Irwin: Without being facetious, throw some back.

Two thousand five hundred yards away on Yong Dong,

the Dukes could see and hear the Black Watch getting the full Chinese treatment. Sam Robertson's machine guns were called into action early in the battle, firing on fixed lines over the Samichon valley and across the Black Watch for over eleven hours. When the order to stand down came and it was time to check ammunition, more than 50,000 rounds had been expended.

A lull in the battle came shortly before midnight. The echoes of the screaming shells continued to whirr in the Jocks' ears like the inside of a conch; but the Chinese infantry appeared to have withdrawn. Half an hour later, however, a bugle blared to announce their return; and once more the crump of grenades and the rattle of Brens and Burp guns punctuated the din of exploding shells. Illuminated by a full moon, countless star shells and, until they were knocked out, the five searchlights of Centurion tanks deployed in support of the Black Watch, the Chinese were plainly visible. According to at least one of the Black Watch they 'were doped. They rushed about madly in all directions and seemed quite oblivious of shells landing near them. They were seen suddenly to stop; no doubt when the effect had worn off.' After the battle opium seeds were picked out of a captured cigarette packet.

Under the pressure of repeated attacks concentrated on a very narrow front the Chinese managed to get a footing on the Hook. Sergeants like Alexander Hutchinson, who led a counter attack on his hands and knees after he had been wounded, corporals like Robert Manning who silenced a Chinese machine-gun with a grenade after being twice wounded himself, and privates like George Coley who bowled Chinese over like nine-pins until he was killed by a grenade, did their best to hold them back. But the Jocks were overwhelmed by sheer weight of numbers and David Rose now decided that a counter-attack was called for. The situation was confused, and for all he knew his men in the forward positions had been annihilated. (In fact, most of them were safe – thanks to Rose's prevision. They had retired to their tunnels and were waiting to emerge as soon as the opportunity was presented.)

Ousting the Chinese from the ground they had taken was obviously going to be no easy task. In an attack down-hill at night the attackers would find it difficult to maintain direction and they would also be silhouetted against the sky. Of necessity the counter-attack would be more in the nature of a systematic and deliberate clearance operation than a mad dash to the lower slopes. In such circumstances Rose believed that the close support which could be afforded by a Centurion tank should prove invaluable. With its searchlight, heavy armament and machine gun, the tank could chaperon his men on to their objectives. As five Centurions from B Squadron, The Royal Inniskilling Dragoons, were already deployed around the Hook there was no question of any delay.

Lieutenant Michael Anstice decided that this was a job for him and shortly after 1 am his Centurion climbed laboriously up the steep slope leading to the Hook. At 1.34 Anstice had reached a position overlooking the battlefield, and the crack of his twenty-pounder shells was added to the rest of the crashing and roaring that was rocking the hillside. Unfortunately for him, however, the Chinese had come prepared for such an eventuality, and a well-placed round from a rocket launcher put paid to any further support for the counter-attack force from Anstice's Centurion. Anstice himself was not hurt, nor his gunner. But the driver was wounded and there was obviously little sense in waiting for other anti-tank missiles to knock out the tank for good and all. Meantime the Jocks had made some progress. With great *panache* Second-Lieutenant Roger Doig had led his platoon in a bayonet charge to sweep the Chinese clean off the slopes of the Hook and back down Ronson. Predictably, the charge failed. Doped or sober, the Chinese held their ground and Doig was killed in a splatter of automatic fire.

When dawn broke about 4.30 am the fighting was still going on. The Jocks were pressing forward; odours redolent of the slaughterhouse pervaded the atmosphere and the whole area was strewn with shattered humanity. No end to the battle seemed in sight. But the Chinese had failed to consolidate their position and they were not prepared to carry on the fight in daylight. So once again the raucous notes of a bugle rang out. And this time they were not an overture to battle but a signal to retire. Not that a withdrawal seemed about to be staged. For while the remnants of the assaulting troops fought a rearguard action, fresh parties of other Chinese suddenly appeared, scrambling up the re-entrants and trotting over to the scene of the fray. Unaware of their role the Black Watch assumed they were reinforcements. 'Situation very confused. Small parties of enemy have suddenly appeared all over the slopes,' 'W' Company reported to Battalion Command Post. 'Have you any reserves left?' queried David Rose. 'No,' replied 'W' company. 'Stick it out,' said Rose.[3]

The new arrivals were battlefield clearance squads. Each was led by a soldier armed with a Burp gun; following him was another soldier wearing a white armband and carrying a pannier of medical dressings. With one exception the remainder were Korean carriers – Gooks [4] – tens of thousands of whom had been impressed into the service of their Chinese allies. The single exception was the last man of each squad, another armed Chinese, who acted as overseer and spur to any laggards. Moving with practised style the clearance squads set about collecting every Chinese casualty who could be moved. Bundled on to stretchers dead and wounded alike disappeared over the lip of the ridge to be trotted back across No Man's Land; only irrecoverable bodies or shattered unrecognizable limbs were left.

[3] The Black Watch rifle companies were labelled W, X, Y, Z instead of the customary A, B, C, D.
[4] The word 'Gook' was frequently used to denote the North Korean enemy. The word was derived from part of a greeting used to the troops by friendly South Koreans. Smiling, the latter would say something that sounded like 'Me Gook'. Later, by a curious transposition of ideas 'Gook' became a synonym for the enemy and the South Koreans became known as 'Rok' (Republic of Korea) troops.

A few of the Jocks had been captured when the forward platoons were over-run, and some of these disappeared with the casualties. Some, like Privates Macdonald and Graham managed to escape. Macdonald, deprived of his rifle, resorted to his fists; Graham split the skull of his Chinese guard with the brim of his steel helmet. But others were not so fortunate. Corporal Wilson, wounded in the knee, narrated his experiences later. 'They took us out of the tunnel, and distributed leaflets to us all. They then searched our pockets . . . I noticed that the Chinese had complete disregard for their own safety, and were walking about and jabbering as if nothing was happening . . . At about 0500 they started pulling out their dead. I saw 40–50 being carried; they worked like Trojans to get them out. At the end one Chinese came along and shook my hand, saying in broken English "Good Luck".'

Daylight brought a conclusion to the battle. Shortly after 6 am Canadians of the Princess Pat's took over from the weary Jocks, the evacuation of the wounded began in earnest, and the butcher's bill was totted up. On the slopes, spread-eagled on what remained of the wire more than a hundred dead Chinese, missed by the Gook evacuation parties, were counted. Twelve Jocks had been killed and 20 other Jocks were missing; one Black Watch subaltern, five other officers and 67 Jocks had been wounded. For the third time the Hook had been held. A month later General West pinned medal ribbons on nine Jocks while the Black Watch pipers wailed. 'Whenever there is a battle,' he said, 'the Black Watch is usually in it, and the Battle of the Hook was no exception.'

4

THE FIGHT FOR INFORMATION

I have been passing my life in guessing what I might meet with beyond the next hill or round the next corner.

WELLINGTON

In defence, says *The Infantry Division in Battle*, 'They [the infantry] must show a real spirit of aggressiveness by harassing the enemy by all means available, such as vigorous patrolling and the offensive use of the artillery and other supporting weapons. The domination of "No Man's Land" must be in our hands.'

By the autumn of 1952 the domination of No Man's Land had become the all important issue in Korea, and from rival outposts of the two stalemated lines patrols fought to probe enemy defences, take prisoners and gather intelligence. Hardly a day or night passed without a clash, an ambush, a brisk and bloody fight in No Man's Land. This was the true subaltern's war, the period which received little recognition beyond the terse official communiques, 'Nothing to report. Patrol activity'.

In the grey middle of the war, when nobody was winning and hope was frozen, the ill-publicized patrol activity was the essence of the U.N. defence. Along the front line of the Commonwealth sector the Chinese and British positions were usually between 600 and 1000 yards apart, separated by a paddy valley. Except when they were on the same ridge, the positions occupied by both sides were almost always on steep slopes. Because the British positions were generally wired in and surrounded by minefields the Chinese correctly appreciated that night attacks were the best way of capturing them. So, to try to anticipate and get some warning of an attack a screen of patrols was thrown forward. According to the nature of their tasks they were dubbed 'fighting', 'reconnaissance' or 'standing' patrols, but all of them had the same aim – to gain information. The role of the fighting patrol was to intercept and destroy enemy patrols and generally interfere and upset; reconnaissance patrols sought to learn about the Chinese positions and habits, and standing patrols were deployed to give warning of enemy approach. Information was priority number one, but whichever side could turn No Man's Land into a stamping ground for its patrols clearly possessed the initiative.

The Dukes arrived in Korea firmly determined to seize and hold the initiative. Ramsay Bunbury, well versed in the importance of patrols in the campaign in Italy, had given much thought to the problem from the moment he learned that his battalion was bound for Korea. He had read the intelligence reports about the experiences of other regiments in the static war – how, more often than not, orthodox patrols of platoon and company strength had either failed or had been only marginally successful in the fight for information; how other patrols had blundered into minefields; and how too vigorous a patrolling programme had worn down men detailed to go out night after night. If it were possible to profit from these reports he intended to do so.

In the early days of November and December, 1952, however, the Dukes were inexperienced, and reality *in situ* was more pressing than ideas *in vacuo*. Nightly, in the relative calm of Yong Dong, security demanded that no less than fourteen standing patrols had to be established as listening posts up to 200 yards outside the wire of the positions. As each patrol was made up of an NCO and four men, the immediate problem was where to find all the men and the reliable and trained NCOs to command them. The feasibility of reducing the number and size of the patrols quickly proved to be out of the question. As the patrols guarded the avenues into the battalion positions, and were supposed to give warning and check any Chinese approach, they were an essential part of the defensive system. Putting a young officer in charge of each was one way of ensuring that they got to the right place at the right time and functioned efficiently, and this is what was done to begin with. But it was soon apparent that junior NCOs would have to shoulder a responsibility which would weigh heavily on the rifle companies. In the event there was surprisingly little difficulty finding the NCOs to lead standing patrols, and the lance-corporals and corporals quickly adapted themselves to the demands placed upon them. Night after night, in rain, frost, snow, moonlight or fog, these young NCOs handled the standing patrols with boldness, competence and quiet efficiency. Giving them responsibility built up their confidence and authority; in consequence they became more effective leaders. Sewing stripes on a man's sleeve does not automatically make him a leader. Before promotion he may have given signs of having the stuff an NCO needs, but unless he has experience in the real exercise of authority he is likely to feel uncertain in his new role. A good deal of encouragement, understanding and experience is required before he becomes an effective junior leader.

The standing patrols were the most vital and the most sensitive safeguards of the British defences. Not only were they the cushions which took the first shock of a Chinese attack, they were also the prying fingers spread out to detect the movements of enemy patrols. So much depended on them.

Fighting patrols, on the other hand, were the manifestation of that 'offensive spirit' considered necessary to counteract the lethargy generated during a period of static warfare. To them fell the task of '*dominating* No Man's Land', that ominous phrase to which allusion has already been made and which is so lightly bandied around the operation orders and directives of all armies. What it conjures up in many people's minds is a popular cinema and television screen image of countless bellicose squads of unshaven, trigger-happy individuals prowling around in specified areas looking for opportunities to 'beat up' similar parties of the enemy. In practice nothing could be further from the truth; in Korea fighting patrols invariably had clearly defined objectives.

As could be expected, every commanding officer, every brigade commander – and for that matter, every general officer in the theatre had his own ideas about fighting patrols. The Americans favoured company-size 'missions' of about a hundred men; some British battalions considered that the platoon, with its established and viable organization, was the ideal; others, including Bunbury, believed that ten was about the largest number of men that could be effectively controlled in what could usually be resolved into ambush operations. Sometimes the patrols would be directed to sites overlooking or blocking routes used by the Chinese, sometimes to tactical features which they would probably visit, and almost invariably the main consideration would be its suitability for the setting of an ambush. How long it would take to get there and back was usually the critical issue. If, as darkness fell, the Chinese beat the patrol to the selected site they would be in a position to ambush the ambush; consequently there was always the grim game of 'catching' the opponent first and the grim afterlight race to do it.

Consolidating the picture of a battalion deployed in the Commonwealth sector of the line at this time, one must visualize a series of localities with observation and listening posts manned by the standing patrols about 100 or 200 yards in front. One, two or even three ambushes might be posted up to 800 yards ahead of them. Reconnaissance patrols might also be operating, either quite independently or using the ambushes as bases. This formidable array was what formed the screen, dominating the ground it held and providing a barrier which the Chinese had to pierce before they could assault the main defences. If they were to pierce it they had first to locate it – no mean task in itself; then they had to fight it – again no mean matter, since all the components of the screen not only fought with their own weapons but could call down powerful and flexible support from guns, mortars, machine-guns and tanks. Indeed, it was not unusual for a whole field regiment to answer the call for fire by an ambush.

According to Second-Lieutenant John Stacpoole, the Dukes' Assault Pioneer Platoon commander:

'Patrols in Korea were rather different from what we were led to expect by our training at the Warminster School of Infantry. There we were given a vision of a careful briefing followed by a launch into the bosom of No Man's Land rather as a Polaris submarine disappears under the ice cap for a silent period; but the Korean version was much more analogous to an air flight, where you were controlled by radio from the moment of take off to the moment of landing, and were told what other aircraft you should find at any time on your flanks. Indeed, when there were enough patrols out on a good night from both sides, with a patrol master (usually a Company Commander from the reserve Company or Support Company) plotting it all from a forward command post, it was rather more like a game of chess where the standing patrols were the pawns, the recce patrols the knights, the smaller fighting patrols the bishops and the large officer-led sorties the queens. The Chinamen were fond of large sorties of forty to fifty, but we either stood by the standard ten to twelve men fighting patrol or – before the Dukes had seen real action – indulged in flamboyant, low-yield Company raids conducted by a reserve Company.

Every evening perhaps two standing patrols would go out in front of each forward Company position, led by a corporal – or on the Hook, where the assignment was so important, a sergeant. They would settle in a trench with a field telephone and a wireless set, some two hundred yards ahead of the defensive wire, to function as the Battalion's antenna. Every thirty minutes they would report back with a soft signal; if that signal did not come, a patrol might be sent out to check on their safety. Each patrol usually did half a night, being relieved at an indeterminate midnight, the second patrol coming in again at dawn.

All other patrols went out and usually in by way of these standing patrols, who then could report back that fact as part of the logging process. As one left the trenches one found a gap in the deep defensive wiring looking like nothing so much as one's image of the chosen people passing through the Red Sea into Sinai as all was held up on either side. These lanes through the wiring were of course watched perpetually by Bren gunners. They often gave way to a similar, though far less obviously marked lane through a minefield where we trod softly in fear of error; for, as so sadly happened once in a while, to tread on one's own mines meant not only advertising the presence of an outgoing patrol, but the loss of perhaps two or three of its members – a disaster which entailed the rest humping them back to ambulance jeeps at the Company Administrative Area and the remounting of the patrol, which, by then, was off schedule and upsetting the chess game.

Once out of these safe-passages, it was a matter of avoiding trip flares, following the telephone line down to the standing patrol dugout, and from there – changing the metaphor – the patrol cast off pilot and moved into mid-stream. The programme was arranged by bounds of some exactitude, worked out in Observation Posts and on maps and committed to memory the day before; this was in enough detail to allow for considerable changes *ambulando* as the game progressed, and the master chessman moved his pieces. The advantages of such tight control were immense and gratefully appreciated by the blithe young warrior who felt himself constrained until he froze in the imminent presence of a forty-man foray and found himself able to whisper his position and theirs and invite the Royal Artillery 4·2-inch mortars to tickle them for him. (There were cases of ten men patrols sinking into the paddy beside a bund and watching one of these big Chinese fighting forays slide past them man by man a yard away – and then do a little whispering on the wireless.)

Out in the valley there were various experiences to lighten one's darkness. One of these was the procession of flares sent up by agitated subalterns wonderng if their bit of wire was being probed. These might catch a patrol plodding in the open and casting lurid silhouettes. Flares were occasionally used for a more benign purpose, for example when a patrol commander had lost his bearings or wanted his homing point pinpointed (indeed it has been known for a patrol dazzled by artillery fire, smoke, fog and strange light, to make its way back to what turned out to be the enemy lines). Another of these was 'artificial daylight' created by aiming searchlights – the little ones of the Centurion tanks, or bigger gunner ones on to hovering cloud; and then a patrol might feel too pinned down by the effect to continue its explorations or too bemused by the curious shadows easily to recognize the terrain. Another of these was the steady nightly programme of defensive and harassing fire tasks undertaken by tanks, artillery, mortars and machine guns. I remember one night finding myself and my patrol immediately underneath a tank tracer high velocity shoot at Chinese bunkers and patrol exits, a shoot plotted by daylight, of course. It was rather like lying on the track as the Flying Scotsman went overhead at full speed spraying out sparks, and the noise was deafening. But then, some nights out were very quiet.

On the face of it the nightly screen was sound tactical common sense. But providing and handling it presented some grave difficulties. First, anything up to 100 men at a time had to be found for it, with the consequent weakening of the main position; secondly, the men concerned had to be both determined, courageous, well-trained and well led, and lastly there was always the risk that in the dark and the confusion of a fight in No Man's Land the wounded or the dead would have to be left behind. (In this respect the Dukes were more fortunate than some of the other regiments. Nevertheless they did lose an officer on the night of the Third Battle of the Hook. Subsequently he was confirmed killed.)

The real trouble about patrols is that they have a cumulative effect, and 'battle fatigue' becomes a problem among those who are committed to them. Many people regard bravery in small matters as a question of self-control. In battle one comes to realize that this is not entirely true. Even a courageous man can in the end be afflicted by what was loosely described in the

Second World War as 'bomb-happiness'. As an example, one battle-hardened and gallant Yorkshire NCO suddenly found that he could no longer face another patrol. He had cracked under the strain. Yet shortly afterwards he showed conspicuous bravery in battle; in different circumstances he knew how to control himself. Courage, bravery in battle, is a strange thing and very often a question of circumstances, it seems. Most cornered animals will fight to the death.

During December a fighting patrol of the Dukes clashed with a party of Chinese in No Man's Land. The patrol was led by a young National Service Officer, Second-Lieutenant Douglas Holland, a taciturn young man with a literary bent, a penchant for the quiet life and sleep in the afternoons, and no interest in the acquisition of posthumous military glory.[1] On a crisp moonlight night Holland led his patrol through the minefield gap in front of one of the company positions into the eerie waste of No Man's Land. Beyond the minefield his men split into sections and started to leap-frog forward along a pre-determined circuitous route across the valley. Until the leading scout walked into what he swore later were two Chinese, progress was slow and uneventful. Overcome by surprise, he did not shoot, and if it was the enemy and not a couple of bushes the Chinese must also have been too surprised to fire at him. Holland halted the patrol and listened; sure enough a stealthy rustling and subdued chatter suggested there was a party of the enemy somewhere in the vicinity. The patrol waited. But when half an hour had elapsed and nothing had happened Holland was beginning to worry about the time – whether he would be able to complete the patrol and get back to the Dukes' lines by daylight.

The order was given to move on; the forward section edged up to the next bound, and the rest of the patrol started to close on it. But before the two halves had linked up there was a

[1] D. J. Holland's best-selling novel about Korea *The Dead, The Dying and the Damned* was based on his experiences with the Dukes.

sudden scurry of activity in front, and men were heard racing round the patrol's right flank. The patrol had walked straight into an ambush.

Holland was the first to open fire. None of the patrol had been in action before, and the men instinctively looked to him for a lead; when he opened fire they followed suit. Hesitating nearly cost them their lives. Fortunately, however, the Chinese were disorganized by the first burst of bullets. But this fact was not apparent in the confusion and the patrol panicked. Within seconds the whole lot of them were sprinting back across the paddy. Not until they were brought to a halt by the wire at the edge of the minefield was Holland able to regain control. The Chinese had not followed, nobody was missing or hurt, and everything was more or less quiet again.

Holland was furious. He knew he could expect little sympathy if he reported what had happened as it happened. 'You've lost the confidence of your men,' he would be told. But in the confusion perhaps the patrol had killed a few Chinese. 'Maybe,' as one of his men suggested, 'the Chinks were more shit scared than we were shit scared.' The only thing to do was to go back and see.

So the reassembled patrol crept back. It was not difficult to locate where the ambush had taken place, but there was no sign of any Chinese; as usual they had taken their dead and wounded with them.

From Holland's version of the action, Bunbury's understanding was that the Dukes had done rather well in their first real clash with the enemy. This confirmed his determination to go ahead with his plan for giving Brigade Headquarters a Christmas present in the form of a Chinese prisoner. As always when a war gets bogged down in static defences, regiments in the line were subjected to clamorous demands for prisoners, and bottles of whisky or extra days leave were promised to all who could bring one in. The Canadians had some success in doing so. The Australians might have done even better, but their aggressive enthusiasm led them to forget it was prisoners and not dead Chinese they were after. Periodically a prisoner was taken – usually in some daring snatch raid. But it was a rare occurrence. In the Chinese army the so-called '3-by-3' system militated against either capture or desertion. Soldiers fought, worked and played in cells of three, with each man watching the other two and knowing that they were watching him. Wherever one went, the others followed – even to the latrine; in battle they fought side by side – helping or spying on each other according to the circumstances. Consequently the opportunities were few and far between for a reluctant Chinese hero to desert or to be taken prisoner without a fight.

Bunbury's plan for a snatch was finalized on 20 December, five days before it was due to take place. On Christmas Eve a patrol of ten men, under command of Second-Lieutenant David Borwell, a National Service Officer from D Company, was to cross the valley to a scrub-covered spur about three miles in front of the British line. This spur was an outpost of the Chinese defences, and known to be occupied. Once the patrol was in its 'base' position, the snatch party proper would detach itself and work its way round the spur, to where a trench linked a Chinese observation post to their main defences three or four hundred yards farther back. While they were doing so U.N. artillery would shell the spur. Then, when the snatch party reached the trench they were to cut the wire, and lay up over the break, ready to pounce. If all went as expected the Chinese would assume the line had been cut by shellfire and one or more sig-nallers would be sent off to repair it. As they came up the trench the snatch squad would have an opportunity to knock one off. But if things did not go as expected, and no signallers material-ized, the snatchers were to stay in position. Somebody was bound to come up the trench sooner or later.

Borwell, a calm and good-humoured young man of medium height, was cast in the same hefty mould as most of the Dukes' subalterns. Intelligent but open-minded, extremely strong and quite fearless, he had opted for the crucial role in the snatching operation – that of coshing the signaller. Corporal Andrew McKenzie, a tough, war-scarred, thick-set Geordie, and his croney Corporal Tom Dickie, were to accompany him. Dickie, a loose-limbed Irishman, and McKenzie had both served as paratroopers, and the latter had expressed his intention of winning the Military Medal in Korea. Between them Borwell, McKenzie and Dickie had all the qualities needed for an operation of this kind, and they were determined to make it succeed. Together they practised coshing a man in a deep trench and pulling him out. Both operations were more difficult than they had expected, but by Christmas Eve Borwell reckoned they were experts.

Last-minute preparations were completed about 8 pm on Christmas Eve, and the patrol filed out into No Man's Land. The gunners on both sides seemed to be taking time off for once. But it was snowing gently, and the ground was granite hard. As the men gingerly picked their way across the stream at the bottom of the valley the sound of cracking ice split the black silence. An occasional star shell lit up the countryside causing them to 'freeze' in its glare, feeling as exposed as Nelson's column would be in the middle of Stonehenge. Tense and anxious they held their breath waiting for the 'Buuurrrppp' of a Chinese sub-machine gun. But they were undetected, and by the time the moon appeared the patrol had reached the place selected as the 'base' location. 'Phase One completed', Borwell whispered into the radio. 'Roger. Well done', came the reply. As the snatch party moved on, the shelling started to fall on the spur, dead on target. Everything was going according to plan. The shelling lifted about 2.45 am and Borwell's party reached their objective about fifteen minutes later. The trench was much as they had expected – about five feet deep and three feet wide, with its spoil humped into a ridge on either side. In both directions it stretched back into inky darkness; there was no sound or any other indication of the enemy. Facing towards the main Chinese positions, Borwell lay down along the edge of the parapet and took a firm grip on his cosh; McKenzie jumped down into the trench and felt for the telephone cable. This, like the British lines, ran along the side of the trench, clipped at intervals to pegs in the trench wall. A quick snip with the wire cutters he had brought for the purpose, and the second phase of the plan was complete. All they had to do now was to wait.

An hour passed and the snatch party grew progressively colder with every minute; then came their big moment. Men could be heard coming up the trench, chattering loudly. And in the light of a distant flare there was a glimpse of two Chinamen feeling their way slowly along the cable and coming towards the snatch party. Then yards from the cut they stopped and appeared to argue. Possibly their discussion centred on the finer points of fan-tan or some philosophical issue raised at their evening study session. More likely they were as irritated at being sent out to mend a break in the line as a couple of British signallers would have been in similar circumstances.

Finally one of the Chinese picked up the wire and moved up to the break. At the cut he shouted to his colleague and bent down to examine the break. 'Now,' yelled Borwell, heaving himself towards his quarry and lashing down his cosh. McKenzie fired a burst from his sten in the direction of the other Chinaman, while Dickie attempted to grab the target of Borwell's attack. But both Chinese got away. In the dark McKenzie's bullets went wide of their mark and as their target bolted up the trench in one direction, Borwell's intended prisoner slipped under Dickie and shot off in the other – off towards the observation post on the spur. The cold had cramped Borwell's muscles and when he struck out, his blow had glanced off the shoulder of the Chinaman's quilted jacket. Twisting away, the signaller had dived underneath Dickie and disappeared like a rabbit bolting up a burrow.

So ended the snatch operation. Once the trap had been sprung there was no point in staying, the Chinese would return to the spot with reinforcements and unless they moved quickly they might find themselves cut off. In the event the return to the base was uneventful. The plan had worked perfectly and the lesson of its failure is a typical instance of a bitter truth of war – that the unexpected can happen and often does.

At this time the opportunities for mounting daylight operations were rare indeed. Both sides kept a close watch on each other and any movement between the stalemated lines would quickly bring down a stonk, the length and concentration of which would depend on the importance attached to what had been seen and how long it continued to be under observation. OPs were always on the lookout for the gunner's dream of close-packed serried ranks tramping through No Man's Land, but they never materialized. By day men kept to their trenches, resting, waiting, watching.

But there was one short period of daylight which offered a slight advantage to the Dukes in their sector of the line during January, 1953. Rising from behind the British positions the sun shone directly into the prying eyes of Chinese observers on the forward slopes of their hills. For about an hour they would be dazzled. By coupling this natural effect to a concentration of artillery, tank and mortar fire Bunbury concluded that it would be feasible to move men into the valley with little risk of their being caught in a retaliatory barrage. Dazzled by the sun, blinded by the smoke and dust and sheltering from the British barrage, the Chinese would not be expecting such a move anyway. For the past three months all activity on the Commonwealth Front had taken place at night.

A decision to put this theory to the test was taken when a series of two-men reconnaissance patrols reported a suitable objective. Opposite, and a mile distant from the hill occupied by 'C' Company of the Dukes, a long scrub-covered spur jutted out from the ridge along which the Chinese had sited their front line. They had an outpost on each side of the spur but, until a reconnaissance patrol reported hearing men digging, the spur itself was thought to be unoccupied. If men were digging, it looked as if preparations were being made to change this. So another patrol was sent out to lay up all day on the spur. When they returned they reported seeing the entrance to a tunnel behind a small knoll at the foot of the spur. This was sufficient confirmation, and on Christmas Eve, while David Borwell's snatch party were attempting to grab a prisoner farther down the valley, a fighting patrol was sent out to have a proper look at the tunnel.

Second-Lieutenant Ian Orr, who with Sergeant Nowell had lain out all day on the spur, commanded this patrol. Orr, a stocky, quiet-spoken and zealous young National Service Officer, was ordered to kill or capture any Chinese he met in the course of the patrol and to see whether the tunnel could be destroyed. In the event, the Chinese working in the tunnel saw the patrol approaching and hastily withdrew back to their own lines. Before they came back in force to deal with his party, Orr had a few minutes to inspect the tunnel. It was quite a sizeable affair and if it were to be destroyed explosives would be needed. Clearly this meant a much more ambitious and carefully planned operation and so the idea of the daylight raid was conceived.

The plan was to cross the valley about 8 am, under the cover of an artillery barrage and a five-minute smoke screen laid by the battalion mortars. On the day prior to the attack a reconnaissance patrol, trailing its coat in front of another hill three miles away, would draw Chinese attention to this false objective and away from the tunnel. And during the real raid the deception would be kept up by another barrage on the false objective. Once across the valley, the raiders would split into two – a covering party which would occupy the knoll at the end of the spur and an assault group to blow up the tunnel and deal with any Chinese they found in it.

Lieutenant Rodney Harms was nominated patrol commander and leader of the covering party, and the frequency of his trips to the tunnel made Orr the obvious choice for command of the assault group. A Sandhurst officer, Harms was yet another of the sturdy, thick-set young men who seemed to gravitate to the Dukes. Hardworking but not dull, and athletic without being too hearty, Harms had sacrificed a University career and a degree to join the army. He and Orr got on well together – a vital requirement in an operation of this kind. Under Bunbury's supervision they and the other members of the patrol started to train for a task that would assuredly make great demands on their physical powers. The tempo of life in static warfare is not conducive to physical fitness, so road and cross-country runs formed part of the daily training routine. A cardboard model was made of the terrain to make discussion easier, and tactics were practised on ground similar to that of their mission. Battle drills were rehearsed until every man could perform them like a robot. First aid, stretcher bearing and the recognition of mines and booby traps and – for the assault group – special instruction on how to use 20-pound explosive 'satchel' charges were also included in this training. There was little likelihood that word of the raid would leak to the Chinese. But to make sure, the operation was given the code name 'Full Moon', and everybody connected with it was led to believe that it was to take place by moonlight five days after the actual date set for it. The patrol themselves only learned of the time and date during the afternoon prior to the raid.

The raid took place on 24 January, and it was bitterly cold when the patrol assembled in the half-light of dawn. Equipment had been kept to a minimum and the men were dressed in combat-uniforms, with peaked caps similar to those worn by the Chinese. Faces had been blackened with mud, and pockets emptied of all papers which might identify a casualty with the 'Dukes'. 'I'll bet you've got some beer hidden away somewhere,' said a sergeant to one man turning out his pockets. 'No, Sarge, but I've got an opener in case we find some over there.' A final check, watches synchronized, and the patrol climbed out of the trench and filed off through the wire into No Man's Land. In the forward control post which Bunbury had set up overlooking the valley, the wirelesses were switched on, and Bunbury with his artillery officer, Major Bill Mackay, settled down to wait.

At eight o'clock precisely the Commonwealth Division's artillery roared out in unison and high explosive started to hurtle down on to the Chinese positions. The smoke followed, and the patrol came into view jogging across the valley, over the stream and up towards the knoll. Beyond them the Chinese ridge was obscured by the smoke and dust of the barrage.

At 8.25 am Harms reported that he had reached the knoll, and five minutes later that the assault group was attacking the tunnel. Shrouded in smoke and guided by the chatter and coughing of Chinese sheltering from the barrage, Orr's men crept up to the tunnel entrance. The opening was about six feet by three feet and seemed to go into the hillside for about ten yards. Orr threw in a phosphorus grenade which was answered by a burst of fire from a burp gun. But as no one came out more grenades were tossed in. Then a sapper, Corporal Ieuan Jenkins, who despite his contradictory names came from Lincolnshire, ran up and pitched a 20-pound explosive 'satchel' charge straight into the tunnel. With a tremendous crash rocks, earth and timber supports were hurled into the air. Nobody knows how many Chinese were in the tunnel, but only one man was seen trying to get away. 'We heard a scuffling in a nearby trench,' Harms said later, 'and saw a Chink. One of the lads fired, but missed, I threw a grenade which knocked him over.'

'Emplacement blown, no prisoners, all occupants blown to bits, we have one dead Chinaman, shall we return?' he radioed back. 'Get back quickly, and bring the dead man with you,' Bunbury replied. The fire plan continued, and the smoke screen thickened, as Chinese mortar bombs began to fall on the Dukes' positions. Chinese reaction had been slow and confused, and their retaliatory fire was scattered and ineffective.

The patrol returned safely and by 9.15 its members were drinking tea and being slapped on the back. In the words of the official communique 'Two officers and fifteen men . . . had . . . carried out a successful raid.'

5

PRELIMINARY PROBE

Agitate the enemy and ascertain the pattern of his move-
ment. Determine his dispositions and so ascertain the field
of battle. Probe him and learn where his strength is abun-
dant and where deficient.

SUN TZU

At the end of January, 1953, American troops of the 2nd U.S.
Division took over the Commonwealth Division's section of the
line, while the division pulled back to rest, reorganize and re-
train. Only the divisional artillery, which remained in action to
support the Americans, was left behind. The Division did not
move far; south of the Imjin and close to the scene of the gallant
Gloucesters' stand, it remained within sound of its own guns.

This was the Division's first breather since its formation
eighteen months before. The incoming Americans, counting the
days to their rotation and lacking the enthusiasm and vitality of
the men they relieved, were not looking forward to a couple of
months in what they conceded was a most active sector of the
line. Temperamentally unsuited and ideologically ill-prepared,
most G.I.s considered the stalemated war to be a futile exercise;
all they wanted was peaceful co-existence until the politicians
organized an armistice. Despite General Van Fleet's concern
about his troops being kept 'sharp through the smell of gun-
powder and the enemy' the G.I.s favoured a quiet life. Aggressive tactics were to them an unnecessary and dangerous pursuit

and in the Commonwealth Divisional area the extent of the patrolling programme appalled them. The 'Briddish' had suffered nearly a thousand casualties on patrols, yet they still persisted in provoking the Chinese. It was unbelievable.

Once out of the line General West's brigades and battalions were pitched into a hectic round of field training and tactical exercises. These quickly dispelled any ideas that the next two months would be spent 'resting', and before April was out what went on in the reserve area was proving so strenuous that some soldiers were beginning to wonder whether freezing in trenches was not preferable to sweating up hills practising a 'war of movement'. In two months a training cycle, which started with individual training and worked up through a series of company and battalion exercises to a brigade manoeuvre, was completed. The individual training was designed to perfect battle procedures and to improve the standard of weapon training, shooting, physical fitness and junior leadership. This included field firing and route marches over hilly country with climbs of up to 2000 feet. To add incentive a divisional platoon marching and shooting competition was organized. Competition was keen and the troops' enthusiasm was most noticeable. Following their experiences in the line, men had come to appreciate the value of professionalism. Lessons were learned and wrinkles collected from other units – British, Australian, Canadian and New Zealand alike. After one exercise a British officer was heard to say, 'I didn't know we were so bad till I umpired the Australians.'

Apart from training, the usual run of kit checks, weapon inspections, make and mend, the construction of ablutions, latrines, soak pits, and all the domestic routines familiar to a soldier took up a good deal of time. As sanitation and preventive medicine are the prerogative of the army medical service as well as surgery of the wound, Captain Ernest Mackie, the Dukes' doctor, was kept busy trying to instil the principles of hygiene into men who had never realized what they meant until they came to Korea. Tinea is rare in Bradford and, when it does manifest itself as foot-rot or ring worm, it quickly disappears with simple treatment. There is no malaria in Britain, where the climate and conditions are not conducive to the anopheles mosquito. Scrub typhus is not known in Europe, and few people have ever heard of the analogous Songo fever, the haemorrhagic disease supposedly transmitted by rats. But these diseases and a host of others flourish in Asia, and it was Mackie's job to instruct the Dukes in methods to combat them.

Mackie, a National Service officer, was fulfilling his N.S. obligation after a formal medical training. Conscientious, diligent and approachable, his charm was enlivened by a dour Scottish humour. Examining a sergeant who wished to re-engage for another six years of regular service, Mackie announced he could 'find nothing wrong'. 'Well, that's all right then,' said the sergeant. 'Ah!' retorted Mackie, 'but I can't see in there,' pointing to the NCO's head. 'And there must be *something* wrong if you want to sign on again!'

The spiritual health of the Dukes was the concern of Padre 'Robbie' Burns, a non-regular Church of England chaplain. His was a frustrating task. Any aggregation of young men in the pink of health offer problems of spiritual man-mastery which are peculiarly their own, and nowhere except in the forces of the Crown are the horses so brought to water. Opportunity for instruction and uplift are thrust on the man and placed in the parson's hands. It is but the gift to create a thirst that is needed, and it is evident that a great opportunity exists for those born with such a gift. Perhaps the generation of National Servicemen of 1952 were more resistant, or those who joined the Dukes less interested in spiritual salvation than the great majority of soldiers on active service. But Burns was presented with one opportunity to demonstrate Christian charity when the Harms-Orr fighting patrol returned bearing the body of a Chinese commissar. Asked if he would say a few words of prayer when the body was interred, Burns declined. 'I couldn't do that,' he said with quiet conviction. To the men present his words sounded like a rejection of an application sanctioning the entry of a heathen into the Kingdom of Heaven.

In camp the troops lived in tents, of which there were two types, the 'Mug' which was a British issue and the 'Squad' which was an American model. On an average both tents held ten to twelve men, although more were sometimes squeezed in by 'double-tiering' the beds. For the most part these were camp beds or improvised creations of signal wire strung between the iron pickets used at the front to support the barbed wire defences. With a sleeping bag and blanket they were quite comfortable – certainly infinitely more so than on the hard ground of a bunker or tunnel. Each battalion also had a variety of individual and original designs of accommodation.

Tents were heated by the same ubiquitous casualty-causers of the bunkers and dug-outs. And the accident rate with these space-heaters was as high in the tents as in the forward areas. A tent, of course, burns down very quickly.

As in the line public utilities such as electric light, water supply and plumbing were virtually non-existent. Water came to the camps in water trucks to be stored in forty-gallon drums. Deep trench latrines, fifteen feet deep and seating six or eight, supplied the plumbing. 'Don't put any antiseptic down them,' Ernest Mackie warned the Dukes. 'It'll only stop the bugs working . . . Best if you take a look every morning. Lift up the lid and get your head well down.'

As the days slipped by and the men became acclimatized to life under canvas, the yen for warm holes in the ground grew less. Camp life was not enhanced by the heavy spring rains which succeeded the Siberian winds. Those who had dug their tents down to keep warm and not provided an adequate drainage system sometimes found themselves in a situation comparable to that of alligators in a swamp.

The training area, being in the battle zone, was situated north of a civilian 'No Pass' line, so the soldiers saw nothing of the civilian Korean community. Thus, in a region where every form of entertainment had to be provided from within the soldiers' own resources, companies and battalions vied with one another in the creation of canteens. Taking their cue from NAAFI, the King's, the Dukes and the Black Watch built pubs. Brightly painted and adorned with hanging signs, *The Supporting Arms*, *The Baker's Dozen, Charley's Bar* and others were places for men to relax, drink Asahi beer, eat chocolate and biscuits, play darts, or just lounge on couches created from sandbags and old beer crates. At sing-songs *Auf Wiedersehen, Sweetheart,* made popular by Vera Lynn – once the 'sweetheart of the forces' – competed with the pop songs of American teenage heart-throb, Elvis Presley.

Nothing is better for a soldier's morale than news from home. Letters from loved ones are eagerly awaited and they satisfy some of the urge to keep in touch with events back at home. The stock of a post-corporal rises and falls more quickly than that of any other person. But letters are not enough; only newspapers can give the overall local picture. Here the Dukes were fortunate in having *The Yorkshire Post* to espouse their cause and sponsor a 'Newspaper for Korea' fund. Contributions and gifts towards the cost of air-mailing the papers out to Korea poured into the *Post*'s offices enabling men on the other side of the world to relax with a glass of Japanese beer and a local newspaper no more than four days old.

For the officers and sergeants, reconstituted central messes served as a home from home with formality reduced to the minimum of that demanded by courtesy. In the Black Watch mess David Rose initiated and led a series of both formal and spontaneous parties with the greatest of gusto. 'Colonel David' was an accomplished raconteur, and his audiences were entranced by a fund of stories which ranged from shark fishing in the Red Sea with a black nannie for company, to fighting duels on the lawns of Gleneagles. Raas Macrae, Rose's jovial second-in-command, was both keen on parties and a social asset when one was in swing. His 'Hi lass, bonnie lass, whar d'ye get the bairn', sung in a healthy baritone, was generally the sign that Black Watch revels were proceeding satisfactorily. With the Dukes' officers the popular rendezvous was a wooden hut, built by the battalion's Assault Pioneers mainly to cater for Ramsay Bunbury's addiction to bridge.

Sergeants' messes flourished on similar lines, and there was a good deal of inter-regimental traffic between them. As in the First World War these messes had their murals; they had moved on since the Kirchner girls, but the message was still the same. They also had plentiful supplies of liquor – to the constant envy of the Americans who still fought the war in a mood of resigned temperance. Many Americans came to the messes as visitors, fascinating and aweing their hosts with a variety of personal weapons. Pistols predominated, worn in tied-down holsters, in positions which the owners claimed specially advantageous for 'the draw'. Knives and daggers were also common, but the most impressive weapon was a tomahawk, whose owner described it as 'a handy little weapon if you get amongst 'em'. In friendly rivalry and a generous spirit of hospitality each of these messes tried to outdo the others; the King's members formed a 'Spike Jones' band, the Black Watch generally had a piper lurking in the background; the Dukes maintained a reputation for vast quantities of beer and good food.

Every unit built a cinema of sorts; films were changed every two nights and such recent releases as *A Streetcar Named Desire*, *The African Queen* and *The Greatest Show on Earth* were shown. In the line a man was lucky if he saw a film once in four weeks. Projectors could be set up for open-air shows almost anywhere, and the projectionists were more than willing to work in the forward areas. But to do so and congregate men within range of the Chinese 122-mm guns was usually asking for trouble.

Concert parties were a rare treat; the heart had gone out of ENSA's show business in 1952 and the famous stars who had given performances freely or for nominal sums no longer came to Korea. 'Ensatainments' were expensive and like other morale raisers their value had, to some extent, to be taken on trust. Not that there were any doubts among the audiences, who welcomed the performers with great enthusiasm while staring at the girls as if they had forgotten such a breed still existed. For the troops, concerts were a tonic for the nerves for which, on occasions, there was no adequate alternative. At one show their stage faced towards the front line, when three miles behind them the guns of the Divisional artillery were called upon to fire a D.F. task. When the guns fired their muzzle flashes were clearly visible to the concert audience, who knew what to expect. But the whoosh of a shell passing overhead and the bang that followed were most disconcerting for the performers, and one singer is said to have warbled to a stop with '. . . many a heart has been bro-o-o-ken'!

Efforts to get back to the standards of peace-time soldiering took various forms. Flagpoles and camps glittered with paint and whitewash, football and hockey pitches were laid out. Who played what depended on the unit, and it was to be expected that the Dukes would concentrate on rugger, risking broken bones on hard and stony grounds. But the Dukes also took special pride in a rudimentary golf course. Nine holes were sited amid trees, streams and wire, and here the enthusiasts came to play using hockey sticks as clubs and whitened fir cones as golf balls. Among these enthusiasts was Major Lewis Kershaw. Quiet-spoken and slightly plump, Kershaw had sandy hair, a small well-trimmed moustache and a full pink-complexioned face in which the features were neatly and evenly proportioned. His general air of comfortable dignity and unruffled calm seemed more in keeping with a successful businessman than a soldier. Unlike four out of five of his fellow company commanders he was not overly ambitious, and the medals and decorations which others coveted had little appeal for him. Kershaw was one who preferred the quiet life; if he could have chosen to be in England or Germany rather than in Korea, no doubt he would have done so. But he was a good officer, who was soon to reveal hitherto unsuspected talents.

With spring in the air the Black Watch returned to the scene of their November triumph. The brown, treeless ridges of the Hook had the same sinister, unattractive appearance, but heavy rain and the first tremulous notes of a few courageous birds gave promise of seasonal change. Out on patrol at least it would not be cold.

After two months of constant and costly patrol actions the American infantry were pleased enough to hand over to the Jocks. The Hook was still a hot spot and the colonel vacating the position painted a grim picture of his men's experiences over breakfast. David Rose listened quietly to his assessment, fascinated by the American's picturesque habit of spitting at frequent intervals and in various directions. The Black Watch knew the Hook and Rose was not unduly depressed by what he heard. Hard work and hard thinking would put things in a more healthy condition and a readjustment of the battalion's responsibilities, sanctioned by Brigadier Joe Kendrew, would help. An adequate defence of the Hook feature required one rifle company to be deployed on each of its four hills – Pt 121 on the left, The Hook proper, The Sausage, and Pt 146, on the right. As four companies forward would mean no tactical reserve to give 'depth' to the position, the brigadier had authorized the loan of a rifle company from the reserve battalion of his brigade – then the Dukes. This company would be deployed on Pt 146, overlooking the Ko Dong tributary of the Sami-chon.

The first of the Dukes' companies to garrison Pt 146 and to qualify for the sobriquet ' 'V' Company, The Black Dukes', was Major Rudolf Austin's 'A' Company. Austin, who at 39 was older and some years senior to the other company commanders had originally been commissioned into the King's Regiment – the third battalion of Joe Kendrew's 20th Brigade. Both his father and his grandfather had been generals. Tall and spare, he was not one of the rugger-playing fraternity. As his carefully groomed appearance, elegance and general air of unassuming benevolence suggested, cricket not football was his game. His clipped moustache, delicate hands and boldly chiselled nose showed some evidence of his connection with the house of Habsburg, whose blood he inherited through his mother.

But while his appearance suggested a sybaritic trend which might have belonged to a connoisseur of art and gracious living, Austin was in reality a most conscientious and delightful individual – easy to get on with and never dull, and possessing a turn of humour entirely devoid of malice. When the Dukes were warned for Korea, Austin, who was then holding a staff appointment in Greece, immediately applied to return to regimental duty and joined the battalion in Pontefract. Bunbury, appreciating that an older and more experienced man would be an asset in the role of battle adjutant, promptly earmarked him for this key appointment. It was not to be. When the battalion sailed for Korea, Austin was hors de combat, recovering from an appendectomy in a Pontefract hospital, and he did not arrive in Korea until December. By this time his wife's cousin, Tony Firth, was battle adjutant and Bunbury had a more pressing appointment awaiting Austin. Major Dennis Simmonds, then commanding 'A' company, had had a hard war in Burma. As Bunbury's adjutant in Germany the stress of the work involved in getting the battalion to war had also had an effect. He was mentally exhausted before he got to Korea and by the end of November it was only too clear that the stress of operations over the next few months would be too much for him. Austin took his place.

By the time 'A' company moved up to Pt 146 Austin had developed a ravenous taste for patrolling. In the normal course of events company commanders were debarred from going out on patrols. According to Rifleman Harris:

It is, indeed, singular, how a man loses or gains caste with his comrades from his behaviour, and how closely he is observed in the field. The officers too are commented upon and closely observed. The men are very proud of those who are brave in the field, and kind and considerate to the soldiers under them.

But neither Brigadier Kendrew nor General West considered patrols were the place for field officers in their middle or late thirties to gain caste. Their job was to command, co-ordinate and supervise the younger, fitter and more agile officers and they themselves were expressly forbidden to 'swan around' No Man's Land on reconnaissance or fighting patrol missions.

Once Austin had settled in and organized the defences on Pt 146, enthusiasm got the better of him and the knowledge that the Chinese were digging caves below the Hook was a nagging worry. The long, low-lying spur called Green Finger east of Warsaw obscured an area where they could work with comparative immunity. Pinpointing these diggings and keeping a sharp watch on their progress was obviously an essential pre-requisite to the planning of their destruction. Worried by the thought of having to order young officers whose eyes were already puffy from lack of sleep to take out yet another patrol, Austin decided to go himself. So far as any operation which entails picking a way across ground where mines have been sown but not recorded and where the possibility of an ambush or head-on clash with an enemy patrol is always present can be described as such, that which he chose to lead was uneventful. Back at his company command post he telephoned Lieutenant Moncrieff to give the routine patrol report. But pride perhaps, or maybe a sense of exactitude caused him to lay undue stress on the exact location of the caves. Over the phone Moncrieff seemed unimpressed. But within minutes of his ringing off, David Rose was on the line. 'Why are you so sure about these map co-ordinates?' queried the Colonel. 'Because I took them myself,' retorted Austin. 'You mean to say,' said Rose, 'that you took a patrol out yourself? Right! You'll be in front of the Brigadier tomorrow morning.'

At noon next day, Austin duly paraded in front of Joe Kendrew. David Rose was there to accuse, and Ramsey Bunbury had been summoned, presumably to speak either in defence or in mitigation. There was no need. The whole affair was seen as a storm in a teacup; Austin had chosen to ignore a brigade order and had to be admonished for it. Xenophon had established a precedent at the turn of the 4th Century B.C. when he pronounced judgement on a similar case:

> When on active service . . . there is small risk that an officer will be regarded with contempt by those he leads if whatever he may have to preach he shows himself best to perform. If further, the men shall see in their commander one who, with the knowledge how to act, has force of will and cunning to make them get the better of the enemy, and, if further, they have the notion well into their heads that this same leader may be trusted not to lead them recklessly against the foe . . . I say you have a list of virtues which make those under his command the more obedient to their ruler.

In modern war recklessness is not for majors: at least that is what Austin's fellow company commanders thought. Following the carpeting at Brigade Headquarters, they addressed a note to Austin. 'Rudolf,' it read, 'we have withdrawn your Union Card.'

Despite the American colonel's gloomy report, the Hook was not turning out to be the combination of Guadalcanal, Iwojima and Okinawa which he had predicted. During the first few days in occupation the Chinese habitually shelled 'Stonk Alley', the supply route leading up the back of the ridge, and a large proportion of the shells fell close to the Black Watch Command Post. This, to the disgust of its occupants, was not regarded by the rifle companies as a matter of commiseration but one of amusement to themselves.

By this time the hill slopes were bright with purple azaleas, and grass and bushes were forcing their way through the tangle of fallen rushes and weeds in the long neglected paddy fields. In many places there was almond and cherry blossom, and soon afterwards acacia bushes were in flower. In the most imperceptible haze of the morning stand-to even the Hook had a certain soft beauty, which – for men brought up in the mists of Western Scotland – had a special appeal. To the Communist 'psywar' experts such nostalgia was another arrow in their quiver. Sweet music, relayed by courtesy of the Chinese People's Volunteers floated across the valley at the evening stand-to. After a trilly rendering of *There's No Place Like Home* and *Loch Lomond* came the warning, 'Hallo, Scotsmen, are you settled in all right? Keep your heads down. Don't go out on patrol ... Do you know we can shell you any time we like? – shells that blind the eyes?'

There was no question about their being able to shell any time the Chinese were so minded. By the beginning of May guns of 122-mm calibre were spouting barrages from deep emplacements in the semicircle of hills – 'Betty Grable', 'Rome', 'Goose', and 'Pheasant' – opposite the Hook. Aware of the possibility that nuclear weapons might be used against them, the guns were kept in tunnels, manhandled out to fire and then quickly pushed back again, safe from U.N. counter bombardment and air attacks.

On 7 May there was a heavy daylight bombardment, and an Auster plane sent up to locate the precise positions of the enemy guns was shot down over Chinese territory.[1] The bombardment continued and by dusk it was apparent that more than the usual activity could be expected that night. The standing patrol on Warsaw was ordered back about 11 pm, when it reported the caves in the re-entrant below its position were filling with Chinese infantry, and David Rose called for artillery concentrations on the Warsaw ridge. His demand was answered by the U.S. corps artillery, 'eight 8-inch guns which went by the suit-

[1] Both pilot and observer escaped by parachute but were captured.

ably emotive name of "persuaders", something beyond our experience, the equivalent of the main armament of a cruiser. Their shells penetrated the ground far more deeply than 25-pounders and then blew up with a comparatively greater explosion.' Seventy-two shells and an hour later when the Persuaders ceased firing, the Chinese appeared to have called off their attack. But at 2 am they tried again.

Advancing along Ronson their approach was detected by the standing patrol there, and the Jocks were ready. Bathed in the light of 60-mm mortar flares and searchlights, the enemy were caught in the cross fire of 'W' company's machine guns on the Hook and those of 'X' company on Pt 121. Meanwhile the 25-pounders of Lieutenant-Colonel Tom Brennan's 20th Field Regiment were pouring proximity-fused high explosive on to the Ronson ridge, and the combined 3-inch mortars of the Black Watch and the Dukes together with the 4·2-inch mortar of the Divisional artillery were slamming down bombs on areas where the Chinese had set up their own mortars. When gunner O.P.s reported seeing Chinese swarming over the Seattle slopes the Turks also joined in, directing the fire of their own supporting artillery on to Seattle.

Having had experience of similar situations when American troops had decided to 'advance' in a rearward direction leaving flank positions exposed and vulnerable, the Turks were anxious not to be caught napping. At 03.15 the field telephone rang the Black Watch Command Post. It was an English-speaking Turk. ' 'Ow many casualties 'ave you?' he asked. 'A few,' replied David Rose. ' 'Ave you withdrawn?' queried the Turk. 'The Black Watch do NOT withdraw!' said Rose in a tone which could leave no doubt as to his determination.

At that moment, in fact, the Chinese were within twenty yards of the Hook's forward trenches, struggling to break through the protective wire apron. Private Cash, seeing about fifty Chinamen coming towards him along Ronson fired 6000 rounds through his Browning at them. He did not count how many Chinese went down. But Private Clark on Cash's right fired 400 rounds from his Bren and claimed to have felled nine Chinese. And Private Petrie, manning a Bren about 150 yards farther along the trench from Clark, fired another 1100 rounds for which he claimed a modest three certains – although, he added, 'I did see three or four other bodies fall down.' 'With seven thousand five hundred rounds,' snapped RSM Bill Scott later, 'I would have expected you to kill off a whole Chinese brigade.'

It was now 4 am. Throughout the action the British guns had continued to pour shells on to all the approaches to the Hook and as the Chinese closed up to the Black Watch trenches the guns followed them in. D.F. was now raining down twenty yards from the Jocks' positions, well within what is regarded as the usual safety limit. From the confused reports he was getting from the men battling on the hill above him it was difficult for David Rose to know quite what was going on. But it did seem that the attack along Ronson had been halted. So now was the time to hit back and administer the *coup de grace* to what remained of the assault force there. Considering that a total of about a thousand shells and mortar bombs had come down on top of them, it was very doubtful whether there were many survivors on that particular hill. But a counter attack might well pick up a prisoner or two and it might also deter another Chinese assault along that particular route. So Second-Lieutenant Ian Baillie was ordered to take his platoon and 'clear' Ronson.

Baillie knew the ground and he opted to carry out his task in three stages. The first was to get his platoon out on to the Ronson ridge. Normally this was comparatively simple as there was a recognized exit from the communication trench encircling the Hook, which was used by outgoing and incoming patrols. Once through the wire the second step would be to secure the standing patrol position some seventy yards along the ridge. Having sat and shivered there on a number of previous occasions, Baillie was familiar with it. From the standing patrol position the third and final stage would be a methodical advance along the ridge, to the junction where it bifurcated into the Seattle and Paris ridges.

The patrol ran into trouble before it even reached the first bound. Six Chinese approaching in the opposite direction sheered off when one of Baillie's Bren gunners opened fire. But at the standing patrol position another 15 quilt-jacketed enemy showed more spirit. Both sides opened fire simultaneously and Baillie's men, who were higher up the hill, showered grenades down on their adversaries. Shooting went on for about five minutes, until another group of Chinese started to shoot up the Black Watch platoon from behind. Either they had crawled round Baillie's left or had materialized from the dip between Green Finger and Ronson. Some of the Jocks faced towards the new threat to return the fire and at least one Chinaman was hit. But a mad rush brought the rest to grips with the Scotsmen and a close quarter slogging match developed. At least part of the mêlée could be seen and heard by Jocks occupying the Black Watch position on Pt 121. Other than hold their fire there was nothing they could do. Meantime, as if to isolate the fight on Ronson, the Chinese shifted the weight of their shelling to Pt 121 and the ridge which connected it to the Hook.

As in the November battle, the Jocks showed themselves fiercely averse to being taken prisoner. Private Quinn, 'jumped' by a Chinaman who leapt on his back, bashed him in the face with the butt of his rifle. Another Chinese, coming to his comrade's aid, was disposed of by Quinn in a process which he modestly described as 'kicking him up'. But when three others approached, Quinn decided discretion might be a better part of valour. 'I didnae mind two Chinkies, but I thought three was over much.'

Private Graham, having had his Bren gun snatched by a Chinaman, took off his steel helmet, smashed the rim across his opponent's face, splitting the man's head open and killing him instantly.

Private McKenzie, Bren gunner of the patrol, was as much concerned about being caught in the British D.F. fire as being captured by the Chinese. His Bren had jammed and 'shells were landing just behind where I was, and an air burst went off right behind me. While I was lying in this trench I tried to clean my Bren and get some of the dirt out of it. Then I saw a Chink coming towards me. "Stop!" I shouted at him. I wanted to take him prisoner, but I was too excited and I pressed the trigger. But the gun was jammed, so I pushed it into him, grabbed him by the lapels and swung him round. He brought his head down as he was trying to jab it into me and his Burp gun swung into my hands. I then turned to get hold of his hair, but it was too short and I couldn't hold on so I hit him on the head with the Burp gun.' So ended any hope McKenzie might have entertained of a bottle of whisky and five days' leave in Tokyo.

It was now 4.30 am and dawn was breaking when David Rose learned that Baillie was in trouble. 'Haddock', the code word bringing down smoke to cover the movement of fighting patrols, was wirelessed back to the gunners, and a platoon was ordered out to Ronson to rescue Baillie's men.

As things turned out it was not necessary. Baillie fought his way back to the Hook trenches, and Second-Lieutenant David Haugh, a Seaforth subaltern serving with the Black Watch, was killed in the rescue operation. Haugh, and another subaltern, Second-Lieutenant Alec Rattray, who had won a Military Cross earlier, were both killed that night.

In the event the battle, which has come to be regarded as a 'probe', a reconnaissance in force prior to the real battle, was almost over. In the grey light of early morning, men could be seen scurrying about on Seattle and Paris and when men carrying stretchers were seen on Ronson, it was clear that the Chinese were pulling back. The Gook clearance squads were allowed to perform their grisly tasks without hindrance but the artillery shifted to the escape routes and fighting patrols were ordered out to bring in any dead and wounded Chinese remaining after the withdrawal.

For a second time the Chinese had failed to shift the Black Watch from the Hook. How many of them died or were wounded in the attempt will never be known. On the other side of the butcher's bill the price paid by the Jocks was surprisingly small for the scale of the action – two officers and three men killed; one officer and nine men wounded. No prisoners were taken on either side. A patrol to Green Finger brought back two wounded Chinese and for an hour or two the members of the patrol had visions of whisky and Geisha girls. To their chagrin, however, the prisoners curled up and died; they had failed to live up to their vows 'to fight bravely for the sake of the people', China and Mao Tse-tung, and no other honourable course was open to a loyal Communist Chinese soldier.

6

THE PRISONER PREDICTS

The whole art of war consists of guessing at what is on the other side of the hill.

WELLINGTON

'Scotsmen', blared the loudspeakers on the evening of 8 May: 'Scotsmen! You only beat off a patrol action last night. In five nights' time you will have something bigger to deal with.' With spiteful emphasis this message was repeated three times. Its theme was clear; the Chinese recognized that they had been defeated by the Black Watch on the previous night, but they would be attacking again in greater strength on 13 May. And the odds were that they were not making an idle threat. Until 13 May, or whatever alternative date they decided upon, an assault force would be assembling, laying up, cleaning weapons and attending meetings called by company commanders and political officers. At these sessions plans for the proposed attack would be discussed in detail and the individual soldiers would be reminded of their solemn responsibilities in regard to the annihilation of the 'vicious imperialist enemy'. Whether 13 May would be D Day was another matter; the attack might come sooner or it might be deferred for weeks. For centuries the classic works of Sun Tzu have provided a basis for the Chinese conduct of war, and Sun Tzu maintained that

All warfare is based on deception. Therefore when capable, feign incapacity; when active inactivity . . . When near make it appear that you are far away; when far away, that you are near.

Radio messages intercepted by Americans monitoring the Chinese wireless nets and deciphered and translated by Chinese-speaking Americans and other intelligence information strongly suggested that something was afoot. Hordes of silent, shuffling coolies were known to have carried countless baskets of supplies up to the Pheasant, Goose, Duck and Crow features facing the Hook, and the wireless intercepts indicated that fresh battalions of Chinese infantry were in the area. An attack seemed inevitable; the only question was when.

Brigadier Kendrew took the Chinese forecast as his planning date for counter-measures. Relieving the Black Watch was the first of these. The Jocks still had plenty of fire in their bellies and no doubt they would have fought as they had fought before if they had been left on the Hook. But the five weeks of constant harassment which had crescendoed into the attack on the night of the 7/8th, had taken a heavy toll. For their successes the Highlanders had suffered about forty casualties and it was becoming evident that they were feeling the cumulative effects of patrolling and lack of sleep. Their year in Korea was almost up; the Royal Scots were already on their way out to take their place and Whitehall had declared that they were to move to another trouble spot, the Canal Zone.[1] The Black Watch was due for a rest.

In Joe Kendrew's mind there was no question about which of his other two battalions should take over the Hook. The Dukes were his favourite regiment; having watched them 'shake-down' and acquire the professionalism of experienced soldiers, he knew that they would show the same determination on the Hook as they did on a rugger field. Other units might put up 'a good show' but the Dukes would win. He was not to be disappointed.

[1] In the event, this unpopular posting, known deprecatingly as 'Number Ten' in local parlance, was cancelled and the Black Watch went to Kenya to fight a campaign against the Mau Mau.

1. Lieutenant-Colonel Ramsey Bunbury, DSO.

2. Lieutenant-Colonel
David Rose, DSO.

3. Lieutenant-Colonel Brennan with Major Bill Mackay who commanded
the Battery which supported 1 DWR in the battle.

4. Company Commanders on first arrival at Pusan in Korea; from left to right Majors Simmonds, Kershaw, Kavanagh and Firth.

5. Major Austin, Kavanagh and Ince.

6. 1 DWR Daylight Raid, 24 January, 1953. This photograph shows the assault group in full battle equipment. Each member of the patrol wore a combat jacket, combat trousers, peaked cap, rubber soled boots(CWW) and short puttees. Every man carried at least one 36 grenade, a first field dressing, a shell dressing and an eight foot length of signal cable. The main group of five men was comprised of three Bren gunners, a stretcher bearer and the patrol commander (Lieutenant Harms). The assault party consisted of a cover group of two Sten gunners, and the Snatch party of four men also armed with Stens and carrying a cosh and an 80 (smoke) grenade each.

7. Yong Dong in December 1952. This trench system and bunker was typical of the ground in the Commonwealth Divisional area.

8. Major-General Mike West, GOC 1st Commonwealth Division (second from left) and Brigadier 'Joe' Kendrew, commander of 29 Bridgade, with the Dukes patrol.

9, 10 and 11. 'Know your enemy' was one of Colonel Bunbury's maxims, and to stimulate interest in Chinese tactics and habits he invented two mythical commanders: Mr Wu, the political commissar, and Captain Wong, a company officer. How Wu or Wong would behave in any given situation was the subject of much discussion. The above sketch was produced by the Dukes Intelligence section. The photographs opposite were taken during the divisional training period which preceded the Third Battle of the Hook. Above, Wu and Wong are aiming at the Dukes Officers' Mess to pay a social call. Below, Colonel Bunbury is introducing the two 'enemies' to the assembled gathering of Commonwealth officers.

12. The battleground viewed from 'The Sausage'. The Hook, occupied by 'D' Company 1 DWR on the night of the battle is on the left.

13. View from Yong Dong looking towards the Hook.

One company of the Dukes was already holding Pt 146, of course. Major Barry Kavanagh's 'C' Company had rotated with 'A' Company, replacing the latter shortly after Rudolf Austin's patrolling drama and, after a month, being replaced by 'A' company again. So at least two of the Dukes' rifle companies knew something of the Hook terrain. Kavanagh, a comfortable, plump figure, had an Army tradition behind him dating back to the Indian Mutiny at which his great grandfather had won the Victoria Cross. As a young company commander in N.W. Europe he himself had already won the Military Cross. Solemn by nature, Kavanagh was quiet, efficient and dependable. In seeking the best for those under his command he was responsible but not over-demanding. Likewise, while requiring keenness and industry from his officers and NCOs, Kavanagh never subjected them to unnecessary and frustrating tasks and encouraged their personal initiative as far as he could.

'B' Company, commanded by Major Tony Firth who had held the appointment originally intended for Austin as Bunbury's battle adjutant, was destined to take over the key positions on the Hook proper. Tony Firth was a model of what a first-class professional soldier should be. Imperturbable in all circumstances, he was alert, understanding and competent; he handled the men under him with sympathetic firmness and his officers with a tact devoid of subservience. He could cope with the unpredictable, was a hard worker, but knew how to enjoy leisure and had in his personality a strong tinge of humour blended with a sense of the ridiculous. Intensely loyal to Ramsay Bunbury, and to regimental tradition, Firth had been brought up to assume that the British always won all wars in which they were involved. If he had any chinks in his armour as a soldier they might have been derived from this belief, and his concern for the officers and men for whom he was responsible.

As his second-in-command Firth could not have had a better man for the job than Captain Phil Evans. A 'Duke for the duration only', Evans had been an NCO before being commissioned into the York and Lancaster Regiment. Squarely built and stolid, he had a personality to match. With Firth's imaginative and bold mentality, Evans's steadiness, reliability and mastery of detail blended to form an effective working partnership, which would prove its worth in the next three weeks.

The Dukes relieved the Black Watch on the night of 12/13 May and they were expecting to be attacked at any time. Since the Chinese propagandists on the loud speaker had boasted that the British would be evicted from the Hook on the 13th, whispers of 'Tonight's the Night' circulated as men stumbled along the communications trenches towards their new positions. It was a phrase which would be repeated with monotonous regularity until 'The Night' finally came.

The change-over was timed for completion by 7 am on the morning of the 13th, but considerable preparation is needed before a relief can be effected in the line, and this had started on 9 May as soon as Joe Kendrew announced that the Dukes would take over from the Black Watch. Who would go where was quickly decided. Major Kavanagh, whose men had spent more time in the line than those of the other three rifle companies, was offered the option of going either to Pt 121 or the Sausage, both of which flanked the Hook. Because it was reputed to receive less attention from the Chinese gunners than Pt 121, Kavanagh opted for the Sausage. Firth's 'B' Company would take over the Hook, Emett's 'D' Company, Pt 121, and Austin's 'A' Company would move into a reserve location about a mile behind the Hook, from where it could be deployed to support any of the other three companies, or the new 'V' Company (formed by the outgoing Black Watch) on Pt 146.

Fortunately there was little enemy activity around the Hook between the time the Chinese attack on 8 May ended and the time the relief was completed. For once enemy artillery and mortar fire was comparatively light, and company and platoon commanders were able to see and reconnoitre their new positions without undue difficulty. Comprehending the capacity and layout of the trenches, dug-outs and tunnels was a simple matter compared with understanding the minefields. In twenty months, approximately the same number of regiments and battalions committed to the defence of the Hook had sown protective minefields on its ridges and forward slopes. Most of these fields had been laid for a considerable time, and the precise limits of some of them were a matter of conjecture. Fences surrounded the known fields, but the heavy shelling of recent weeks had played havoc with them. Having done their best to put the fences in order, the Jocks organized a series of patrols, round the mines and through the gaps, for the subalterns and sergeants of their respective relieving companies. Where the gaps lay was important because they were the only means of access to No Man's Land; being known to the Chinese they were natural targets for ambush patrols and mortar fire.

The Black Watch handed over the plan of their artillery D.F. tasks in toto. In a static war, against an enemy with manpower to spare, the defensive fire of supporting weapons is of the utmost importance to the infantry, and the one for the Hook was pre-arranged in the greatest detail. David Rose had organized his artillery fire like the orchestra for a Wagnerian opera. (If the music he arranged would stand comparison with that of *Die Walküre*, that of his successor could more closely be represented by *Götterdämmerung*.) Every company commander in the Hook defences had a map with an overlaying trace of the pre-arranged tasks. This enabled him to bring the co-ordinated effect of artillery, mortars and machine-guns to bear on any attack at very short notice or to say quickly whether the fire on any particular task would endanger his patrols.[2]

Other considerations which had to be taken into account before the relief was effected included counter-attack tasks and the roles of supporting arms other than the artillery. Until new

[2] Opinion as to the best method of doing this varied. The Black Watch company commander on the Hook had all the tasks plotted by Code names. Major Firth opted for numbers with a legend at the side of his map showing the Code names.

counter-attack plans were devised those produced by the Black Watch had to suffice and the incoming platoon commanders had to familiarize themselves with these plans and reconnoitre the ground.

More important was to tie in the support of the Centurions of the two troops of 'C' Squadron, 1st Royal Tanks, dotted about in platoon positions round the Hook. These tanks now came under command of the Dukes and what they would do in an attack was a matter which needed to be discussed. Properly used, their 20-pounder guns could be a valuable adjunct to the defensive programme. But their power to ensure that only in those positions which they could not see could Chinese weapon pits and bunkers exist, was sometimes regarded as a doubtful advantage. Infantrymen are inclined to give more prominence to the disadvantage of having lodgers in their positions which attract so many enemy shells. Moreover, so far as Emett's company was concerned an unfortunate incident in January had been forgiven but not forgotten. In the grey morning light a Centurion had embarked on the systematic and highly dangerous destruction of 'D' company's reserve platoon defences. The tank commander, a newcomer to Korea, had misaligned his map and interpreted movement on the ridge opposite his position as Chinese activity. What he saw as an exceptionally opportune target were in fact some of the Dukes doing their morning chores – sweeping the trenches, washing socks, to-ing and fro-ing to the latrines. Round after round of 20-pounder HE was fired at them. Stopping the destruction was no easy task. Having identified the source and relayed the information to Emett, the problem was getting a message to the rogue tank. With no direct communication, the only way was to telephone Bunbury's Command Post, and get somebody to talk to Brigade HQ over the telephone or wireless. The Squadron Commander lived at Brigade HQ and he could speak directly to the tank on his own wireless net. At each stage in the chain of communication individuals had to be convinced that the frustrated recipients of the shells were not mistaking Chinese artillery for the tank gun. (Shells from friendly artillery dropping short has been a common complaint of infantrymen of all nationalities ever since the gunners took to indirect fire techniques. Sometimes, not very often in Korea, they were right. At another time, Andy Lamont an extrovert FOO of the 20th Field Regiment, managed to put a shell squarely on top of Tony Firth's company cookhouse when ranging on a D.F. task.) In such circumstances Sod's law invariably comes into play.

Defence works usually produce an accommodation problem. The incoming platoons of Dukes were slightly stronger than those of the outgoing Jocks and, according to the way it is looked at, there had to be some squeezing and stretching until new bunkers and weapon pits could be dug. In situations like this, defence stores such as wire, pickets, corrugated iron and wood for revetting are left behind for the relieving unit; no signatures are required. Reserve rations, machine guns, and some of the communications equipment are a different matter. Signallers from the Dukes spent three days with the Black Watch before the move, learning the layout of the telephone cables, taking over the stores and settling in. On the 13th all telephones and the company battalion exchanges on charge to the Black Watch were left in situ, while the Dukes handed over an equivalent amount of equipment; both battalions kept their own wireless sets.

Came the night of 12 May, trucks ferried the Dukes up to the rear of their respective hills. Vehicles moved according to a schedule planned by Major Hugh LeMesurier, Ramsay Bunbury's adjutant. Fresh from the Staff College, operation orders flowed easily from his pen, and the relief ran smoothly. Near the Hook battalion Command Post the vehicles stopped to allow the incoming Yorkshiremen to get out, and then moved on to an embussing area to pick up the Jocks. This was done to maintain a one-way flow of traffic.

'I remember that night journey up to the line as no other experience,' John Stacpoole has recorded.[3] 'For there was none other like it. Till then, we had tasted action only watered; but this time we knew with a bracing certainty that we had to face it undiluted, with the veil removed. As we drove up in our columns in carefully planned order, equipped and briefed for a phased night take-over, I remember thinking that we would not see freedom again until we had tasted steel, and that some of us (I felt certain that I would be among them, and so I was) would not come off that hill on our feet, but on a stretcher. It was a fresh May night, moody with moon and cloud, throwing up alternate darkness and dimness, the paddy fields and slopes beginning to burgeon and give off the scents of late spring. I remember, as we motored on without lights, that I said my rosary for my men, knowing what was before them; and as I prayed, there came to me the picture of a trained and sensitive hand in a velvet glove sliding silently into the tempered steel that made of it a mailed fist. Before it was withdrawn again, it would punish and be punished.'

Company by company, the forward platoons were relieved first, so that if the Chinese sprang a surprise a reserve platoon of Black Watch would be available to deal with it. Platoon guides found by the Highlanders met the incoming platoons as they left their vehicles and let them up to the platoon positions. There the platoons were met by section guides found from men who had spent the previous 24 hours in the position. These guides led the sections to their weapon pits, where the outgoing Jocks were standing-to, with men wearing or carrying everything they had with them. 'What's it like?' asked the Dukes. 'Bluddy awfu',' replied the Black Watch.

In fact nothing really bloody awful happened that night or for another four days. Every effort had been made to conceal the relief from the Chinese. The Black Watch formed the patrols on the night of the 12th/13th, and Black Watch operators continued to man the wireless, so that if their frequency was being

[3] Letter to the author.

84

monitored the change from Scottish brogue to Yorkshire dialect would not be detected until it no longer mattered. Four days of comparative peace and quiet enabled the Dukes to settle in and organize their routine. Every night might still be *the* night, but the apparent absence of Chinese aggressive activity suggested the promised attack had been deferred. Perhaps it had been called off. Taking advantage of this situation, the Yorkshiremen, assisted by Captain George Cooper's sappers, worked like beavers to improve the defences. Bunkers were strengthened, communication trenches were deepened and more barbed wire was strung out in front of the weapon pits. The sappers' work was vital. Under the most impossible conditions they constructed the most sophisticated defences – lugging great pillars of concrete and huge baulks of timber up to the forward positions to reinforce the strong points and observation posts. Throughout the month of May, they were out every night, week in week out; when the Dukes replaced the Jocks, Cooper's REs soldiered on. They were a Hook institution, and the Dukes were lucky to have them.

Emett's 'D' Company on Pt 121, entrenched opposite Betty Grable, constituted the end of the British line, and the left flank of the Commonwealth Division. The Turks who had been so concerned about the Highlanders' ability to hold the Hook were still ocupying the next hill. Between the two features a contact position manned mutually by Turks and Dukes and linked by telephone to both battalions was established. Neither could speak the other's language, but a code was devised enabling either to call for supporting fire from the other – mutual assistance which was to prove invaluable in the days to come. On Pt 121 Emett drove his company hard in a frenzied digging programme of new bunkers and weapon pits. 'Dig or die,' he thundered at the troops: 'more bloody sandbags, and more timber,' he shouted down the telephone to Hugh LeMesurier.

On the Hook itself the forward posts covering the most likely approaches from Ronson, Green Finger and Warsaw were occupied by 5 Platoon, under command of Second-Lieutenant Tom Rothery. A telephone connected each section to platoon and company headquarters and this communication system was doubled up with No. 88 wireless sets. The men of these sections were the eyes and ears of the whole defence and theirs was an unenviable task. Rothery's Black Watch predecessor had been killed two nights before he took over and his successor was to be killed two days after he handed over.

Major Kavanagh's men on Sausage were also digging hard.

So too were John Stacpoole's Assault pioneers whose job it was to build the fighting bunkers:

'These were of two kinds . . . essentially the same – a large one for machine guns and a smaller one for LMGs, both provided with concrete lintels above and below the firing slit, 12×14 inches thick.

The first task was to dig a very considerable hole on a forward slope, enough to erect a wooden framework 6×6×7 feet high inside it, with a backfill of six feet of earth to be put upon its roof afterwards. So we began by removing 13 ft of earth a fathom across (several tons of it) in face of the enemy! Half of the earth had to be thrown somewhere but not forward down the hill where the field of fire of the weapon was to be carved out later on; and the rest had to be retained for backfilling to provide a shell-proof roofing above the timbered ceiling of the bunker. The digging of these was done by teams of about four, drawn either from the Company on the position or from Assault Pioneer sections in as much as they were available. Because, at least when the hole had not reached the height of a man, the diggers were visible to the enemy's naked eye, the main digging had to be done in shifts through the night; in the last stages, if the position was not too exposed, the digging could be done by day shifts when the ground could then be seen as it was picked away at. But there was always the risk that daytime digging would call down mortar or artillery fire – and a bomb or shell into so confined a space does not leave a pretty spectacle. Indeed, after the Hook battle, I found myself in Seoul military hospital in the bed next to a nineteen-year-old platoon commander who had been caught in such a confined space: he had 105 pieces of shrapnel in his body and was covered with splints and bandages except for his mouth and eyes. My Assault Pioneers had a healthy imagination about this risk, and when shelling began used to beg to be relieved further digging that day on condition that they would put in equivalent time at night. And night had its agonies too, which included harassing shelling and patrol probing. But hard pick swinging against rock by the light of a blue-dimmed torch is always a good antidote to both fear and cold.

The timber of the bunker structure was brought up to the Company administrative area by vehicle in good time, and from there it was transported along the trenches by day (or sometimes over the top by night) timber by timber to the site. Groundsills were laid with some precision, using levels and set squares. Then the 12×12 inch uprights were lowered into place and secured by cross bracings and further internal sills. In due course the concrete lintels were brought up to be lowered into place above and below where the fighting slit was to be, and that was a task of no small exertion, for that amount of concrete was heavy: it usually had to be humped over the top of the position with rope slings at night along a path previously taped out through wire, picket and other obstacles. It needed a good deal of perseverance and exactitude to settle these perfectly into place under such circumstances.

Finally, the roof was put on, the whole was further braced with roof sills and struts, and earth was poured back on top of it, so that it would withstand 4-inch mortar and 25-pounder direct hits a few times. (During the night of the main battle, every one of these bunkers was hit more than once: indeed every area of ground of the size of a Centurion tank – including the tanks on the position – received an average of four direct hits by shell or bomb.) The last task was to make this new edifice useful by carving out in front of it a field of fire down the hillside which dropped away before it: and, as the slit was by then some six feet below roof (i.e. ground) level after the backfill, this had to be done by carving out what looked like a miniature of a Southern Railway tunnel emerging into a steep cutting which fell away sharply on both sides. Those who know the crusader castle fighting bays, as in Kyrenia Castle (Cyprus), will have gathered the impression this created.

The entrance to the fighting bays gave into a connecting trench of some feet depth by way of an ascending dogleg, semi-tunnelled as it sank to the bunker's floor level thirteen feet down. The fighting area to the front of the bunker was then given a dissuasive coverage of pickets and dannert wire, so that attackers should not get too near with their explosive charges. If and when they did achieve that, and a satchel of explosives blew up inside, the effect was rather horrifying because the whole design of stress had been developed to withstand external pressures, not internal.

Inside these bunkers life could be made not uncomfortable for, say, four men. Little shelves could be fitted between stress beams to tuck away ammunition, grenades, tinned food, clothes and perhaps a framed photograph or two. Old sacking or sand-bags could be nailed to the walls or strewn over the earth-rock floor. Sometimes, to reinforce the whole structure, the areas between beams were packed tight with sandbagging, and that rather considerably reduced space to tuck things away. Camou-flage nets and blankets might be hung over the entrance slit at appropriate times to keep out the weather. Only when it rained were those bunkers miserable to live in, for they were inclined to become water catchment areas.' [4]

The end of the respite came on the night of 17/18 May when the Chinese returned to the Hook. Shortly after 11 pm that night reports started to flow in from the Dukes' standing patrols that the Chinese could be heard chattering and some-times seen moving on all the spurs leading into the Hook. As they approached the Dukes' patrol outposts on Ronson, Green Finger, Warsaw and Long Finger, artillery D.F. was called down and the patrols went into action with their own weapons. Twenty-nine-year-old Lance Corporal Herbert Bailey, an ex-merchant seaman from Manchester earned the Military Medal that night. With two British soldiers – Privates Dodd and Miller

[4] Fr Alberic Stacpoole.

88

– and two 'Katcoms',[5] Bailey was in charge of a standing patrol on Long Finger when it was attacked by about twelve Chinese. When the patrol opened fire three of the Chinese were seen to fall, but the rest took cover, returned the fire and hurled grenades at Bailey's position. Owing to a misunderstanding, due to their being unable to understand the weird phrases, embellished with the usual copulative adjective, of Bailey's orders, the two Katcoms ran back to the main position. Seeing the Katcoms had made off, Bailey ordered his other two men to get back while he covered their withdrawal. As they withdrew the Chinese turned to rush him. Bailey had been shot in the hand, but he managed to hold them off with his Sten and when his ammunition was exhausted he rolled down the spur to get out of the way. In doing so he got away, although he lost his gun. For several minutes he lay still and quiet, listening to the Chinese moving about and talking above him. Then when it seemed certain that they had lost interest in him Bailey crawled back to the top of the ridge, where the Chinese were collecting their casualties. All that was left to him were a couple of grenades and these he hurled before diving for cover again. That was the end of the fracas; the Chinese retired and Bailey crawled back to his own lines.

For an hour or more the situation on the forward slopes of the Hook remained confused; what was happening did not point to an attack but the Chinese were obviously out in strength. By 2.30 am, however, all seemed quiet, and Tony Firth ordered a patrol under Second-Lieutenant John Ingram to 'sweep' the Ronson ridge. Ingram moved out through the minefield, but he had progressed less than fifty yards when he ran straight into an enemy patrol. Both sides promptly went to ground and lobbed

[5] 'Katcoms' were South Korean soldiers attached to the Commonwealth Division as combatants – as distinct from those employed as labourers. Two Katcoms were attached to each rifle platoon section, with whom they lived, fought and fed. One British infantry soldier outlined the situation when he said: 'Our section is commanded by Sergeant Smith, who has under him me, Jones, Robinson, 'Daisy' Bell, Brown, Ferguson, Wu and Wong.' (*First Commonwealth Division* – Barclay.)

grenades at each other. Realizing that the Chinese outnumbered him and that they showed no signs of retreating, Ingram decided that it would be suicide to carry on with his operation and he withdrew. The Dukes did not get away unscathed, but the Chinese had suffered more.

That they had sustained casualties and had not enjoyed the experience became evident next day. For on 18 May the unexpected happened. Just before 5 am a small and unarmed Chinese, his face wrinkled in a conciliatory smile, walked up to 8 Platoon's position on the Sausage.

He was spotted simultaneously by three of Barry Kavanagh's soldiers, all of whom claimed him as their prisoner – the reward of five days' leave in Japan for the apprehension of a live and breathing soldier had not been rescinded. All three made a concerted grab, and Private Hua Hong of the 2nd Battalion of the Chinese 399th Regiment became a prisoner. From 8 Platoon's position he was escorted back to company headquarters. 'How're we placed for some Tokyo leave now, Sergeant-Major?' the escort asked the CSM. 'I'll see you get some leave all right,' replied CSM Harry Randall grimly. He had not had any leave in Japan himself, but he knew what men were likely to bring back from Tokyo. Ernest Mackie, the doctor, had already had to deal with some cases of what was jovially known in Germany as Veronica Dankeschön.

Meantime Hua Hong was proving surprisingly quiescent and co-operative. He had deserted, he said, because he had no desire to continue in Mao Tse-tung's service. As a former sergeant in Chiang Kai-shek's Nationalist Army, Comrade Hua's political officer considered him unreliable and had hounded and scolded him for 'bad thoughts'. Promotion had been denied because of his political shortcomings. Yet the military skills he had acquired put him in a class above the majority of the illiterate conscripts in his unit and when it came to fighting Hua Hong was expected to set a brave example. Apart from an 'honourable' death there was little he could look forward to. In many ways his daily routine

had been much the same as that of a British soldier in the line:
6 pm until 4 am digging and patrolling; breakfast at 4 am and
sleep from 5 am until noon. But while the British National
Serviceman could look forward to demobilization and a return
to civilian life, Hua Hong was committed for the duration of a
long war against imperialism. His prospects of leave were almost
non-existent, and even the limited amount of his 'free' time –
about five hours in every week – was not his own. The Dukes
could write letters, read the *Yorkshire Post* and re-live nights
out in Minden, Pontefract or Leeds; Hua Hong and his comrades had to spend their time receiving political instruction. If
he gave vent to his feelings one or the other of his two companions would be sure to report his outburst. A British soldier
could refer to his sergeant-major as a fascist bastard without fear
of repercussions; in a Chinese unit a remark like this would
never be tolerated.

The information given by Private Hua Hong was that a full-
scale attack on the Hook was imminent and that this time the
Chinese were coming to stay. The attack would be made on the
five hills which the Dukes were defending (two on the Hook,
two on Sausage, and Pt 146), with five assault companies from
the 397th, 398th and 399th Regiments of the Chinese Peoples
Liberation Army. Three other companies from the 399th Regiment would follow up to take over and hold the captured
positions. The assaulting infantry, Hua said, had been specially
trained and they would advance up the re-entrants between
Long Finger and Warsaw, Warsaw and Green Finger, and
Green Finger and Ronson – to within about thirty yards of the
west of their objectives, and then rush the British positions. If
Hua was right, and he seemed to know a good deal about the
forthcoming attack, the Chinese would outnumber the Dukes by
something like five to one. Moreover, their method of approach
would guarantee them relative immunity from the existing
planned concentrations of artillery fire.

Only one secret now remained – the date.

7

BUILD-UP

---

*It is extremely important to keep the enemy in the dark
about where and when our forces will attack.*

MAO TSE-TUNG

After 18 May tension on the Hook steadily mounted. As the
shelling thundered into a new phase of bombardment the trickle
of casualties swelled into a stream and the Chinese grew more
bold. Parties of them took to moving around in full view of the
defenders by day and at night their patrols were constantly
probing the Dukes' positions. The Yorkshiremen watched and
waited, hands gripping weapons, nerves stretched to breaking
point, eyelids drooping with the effort to stay awake.

At the battalion command post, the Intelligence Officer,
Sergeant-Major Corke, tried to piece the unrelated reports of
stonks and patrol actions into a concise and coherent intelligence picture. Bunbury needed this to formulate his plans
economically and safely. Missing, unfortunately, was the one
vital fact for completion of the battle jigsaw, a firm indication
of the timing of the forthcoming attack. And this eluded him
until well past the eleventh hour.

In many ways Corke was an unusual choice for Battalion IO.
In modern warfare against enemies as ruthless and efficient as
the Communists invariably are, no commander can afford to give
less attention to the intelligence side of his plan than he does to
the operational and administrative sides. If he does, he is neg-

lecting to secure detailed knowledge about his enemy and is thereby directly responsible for risking the waste of life, limb and material – not to mention defeat. Thus the job of the IO is a key appointment usually reserved for an exceptionally bright senior subaltern. And Corke was a senior warrant officer, a drill fanatic of the new era – a hard, tough, guts-and-gaiters soldier. With another man the unspoken gap between commissioned and non-commissioned officer would have been adversely reflected in the IO's work. But Corke was exceptional. In the Second World War he had been an officer himself, but he took great pains to be absolutely correct in his relations with his commissioned seniors. To the task of checking and analysing intelligence information he brought the same dedication as he displayed on the barrack square for perfection in drill movements. Inevitably his fierce dedication brought differences with RSM Pearce. Pearce, with his walrus moustache, looked and was a soldier of the old school – a father figure with orthodox views on the way things should be done. (On a battalion drill parade his standard comment was 'Ragged'.) Stolid, stable and kindly by nature Pearce did not approve of the new type of warrant officer represented by Corke and in the dug-out where he presided over a tiny sergeants' mess, Pearce and Corke shared a love-hate relationship. Over a drink or a snack during spells off duty Corke would sometimes air his opinions of the intelligence picture. When he had reached a point where Pearce had heard enough the RSM would stand on his dignity, and Corke's monologue would be stilled by the sharp request, 'Stop talking shop in the mess, Sergeant-Major'.

With rats scurrying round the bunker the implication that peace-time standards of mess conversation and behaviour must be adhered to probably seems incongruous. But the whole situation was riddled with incongruities. On one side of a range of hills men did everything to conceal their presence; less than a mile away on the other side of the same hills their fellows moved along tracks signposted with regimental crests and splashed with whitewash. In the absence of an air threat from Mao's 'celestial eagles' there was even a helicopter pad, a regimental banner fluttering from a flagstaff close to the battalion command post and a posse of smartly dressed regimental police to direct a regular flow of visitors to the 'sharp end'.

Men with experience of other campaigns could marvel at the quantity and quality of the rations in the front line. Food is always one of the main preoccupations of fighting soldiers, and in Korea there was enough to cater for the near fastidious. Generous American rations, supplemented by tea, filled the stomachs of ever-hungry Yorkshiremen. Since the early days in Yong Dong when their stomachs had gagged at half-cooked turkeys dissected with an issue shovel, they and their cooks had acquired the know-how of active service. Every man got a bottle of Asahi beer a day, and most looked forward to the evening tot of rum.

> They try to tell us there's no rum,
> But we've just seen the f . . . . . come,

ran a ditty concocted by the Mortar Platoon.

As the forward area was under constant observation, food, ammunition and other stores were moved up under cover of darkness. After dark a procession of carrying parties would make their way along the trenches laden with ammunition boxes, barbed wire, pickets, food containers and a host of other necessaries most of which seemed to catch on the many protuberances that projected from the trench walls. Korean porters, non-combatants handled by the Quartermaster in the battalion 'B' echelon area, carried most of the stores to the top of the hill. Industrious and for the most part uncomplaining, they were an invaluable asset. Few of them understood more than a few words of pidgin English, and in typical fashion individuals were known to the troops by nicknames like 'Farter', 'Wall-eye' and 'Rumbler'.

Neither the dug-outs nor the trenches were the neat, tidily

built structures which John Stacpoole's account may lead some to suppose. The effects of shell-fire and subsidence were repaired during the hours of darkness, but the erosion of shell splinters, mortar bombs and bullets on the outside and traffic on the inside often gave the trenches the appearance of shallow ravines through a rubbish dump. Under such conditions it is desperately easy for everything to get dirty and disorganized and for men to get tired and dispirited and to give up the effort to do more than just exist. To overcome this a daily routine had to be evolved and rigorously observed. Every man had to know which of the various jobs fell to him and when he had to do them. Trenches and dug-outs had to be spotless. (The Dukes even used to brush the floors with home-made brooms.) Rubbish had to be collected and taken back by the porters to the rear areas for disposal. (Tins were buried; empty beer bottles, in great demand in Seoul, were sold, and the proceeds used to swell the PRI's troops' comforts fund. These comforts included luxuries like mirrors.)

Not all units in Korea had the same standards as those of the Dukes and the rest of the Commonwealth Division.

'Other regimental systems differed from our own so completely as to bewilder us. The officers, even the Commanding Officer, were seen queuing with the rest in the chow line (as though they were not trained and paid more highly in order to use their time better than that); sergeants quarrelled with their officers and private soldiers with their sergeants, seemingly without it being considered a serious breach of relationship; emotionalism appeared to run high, resulting in nervous outbursts about shares of food and drink, or whatever was being divided; the wearing of uniforms became not merely desert-fashion (which was an exercise in panache, after all) but slovenly; and food tins were scattered at random over the platoon areas or tossed into the wire defences to rot under the defender's noses, attracting flies and rats. None of this occurred for long in any unit of our Division, which had scrupulous regulations especially as to the disposal of food and food containers (always a mark of discipline for an incoming unit).

We lived for the most part out of the hand of Uncle Sam, eating up his C7 field rations. 'All this, and C7 too!' was the cry. They were self-contained food packs grouped in a series of tins to cover the meals of the day and such small items as salt tablets and matches. The puddings, for instance, alternated between Mom's treacle stodge and sliced fruit cocktail, supposedly for cold days and hot. An advantage of these was that we could husband away some spare for dark moments of hunger in the middle of a night of digging or mine laying. We did of course get these tins supplemented by fresh food; and indeed on the great days of Uncle Sam's calendar, like Thanksgiving Day, we suddenly found ourselves feasting on turkey. Our life in the line, then, was punctuated either by the familiar quartermaster's meal out of billy cans served by a flickering torch, or brew-ups in our dug-outs on portable solid-meths cookers.' [1]

Latrines and urinals had to be kept in a scrupulously sanitary condition. Most of the former were sited behind the hill and once a man reached the thunder box he could relax and relieve himself in conditions of reasonable security. To get there, however, could mean a hazardous journey along the communication trenches; nor was it feasible or desirable for all the occupants of a weapon pit to be stricken with a simultaneous urge. Urinals were let into the walls of the communication trenches, so they did not present the same problem.

To pursue this unsavoury topic further, the only places where the ground was suitable for digging latrines had been exploited by previous occupants and its disturbance by shell fire contributed to the distinctive odour of war in which the Hook garrison lived. To overcome this problem, the Black Watch and the Dukes installed portable chemical 'kazis'. Keeping these and the desert-rose urinals in sanitary condition required the constant vigilance of the company seconds-in-command, whose task it

[1] Fr Alberic Stacpoole MC.

was. On the Hook, claimed Captain Tony Sherratt, the daily inspection ritual was a great socializing influence.

Primary functions aside, the hardship of dirt is very real to the sophisticated soldier of today, coming from a high standard of living. Up to about the turn of the century British soldiers came from humble homes with few amenities, where washing, sanitation and hygiene were rarely practised or known, and the dirt experienced on active service was not greatly dissimilar from the conditions from which they had come. But in the twentieth century there are few men who do not shave once and wash twice a day, and have a bath at least once a week. To them the hardship of dirt is in great contrast to the lives from which they have come and it causes considerable discomfort and lowers morale. Even on the coldest days the British troops in Korea stripped to the waist to wash, and every man was sent back down the hill once a week to get a proper bath at the mobile bath unit in the battalion 'B' echelon. Alternatively he could visit the improvised bath-house below the Command Post, where a Korean custodian supervised an ingenious contraption of forty-gallon drums where water heated by a petrol burner supplied the shower.

There can be little doubt that this strict attention to hygiene paid handsome dividends. Cleanliness, foot-powder, DDT and the malaria-suppressant paludrin kept disease at bay, and made life more liveable in Korea. As a result the main drain of casualties was restricted to those who were killed or wounded in action. Between 10 May and the start of the Third Battle of the Hook on 28 May the Dukes suffered fifty casualties from artillery and mortar fire. Most of these were wounded and thanks to the life-saving medical services the greater proportion survived. Knowing that he will be well looked after if he is injured bolsters a soldier's morale and in Korea the medical and hospital services were second to none. Behind Ernest Mackie's regimental aid post were facilities which were as good if not better than those available in Britain. Helicopters evacuated emergency cases where speedy attention often meant the difference between life and death or the loss or saving of a limb. In less than an hour the 'choppers' could make the trips from the pad behind the Dukes' regimental aid post to a U.S. Army MASH (Mobile Advance Surgical Hospital) and in five minutes they would be on the operation table. In what was one of the deadliest wars for citizen-soldiers this was de luxe treatment.[2]

Despite the facilities for rushing the wounded to the hospitals, it was inevitable that some casualties would be beyond medical help. The task of patrolling was both monotonous and deadly – monotonous in its dull routine and deadly in the slow but steady toll of casualties it claimed. No matter how cautious brigadiers like Joe Kendrew, and battalion commanders like Bunbury and Rose, might be in risking lives unnecessarily, Chinese artillery fire caused the list of dead and wounded to mount. The price of a year in Korea was roughly the same for every infantry regiment: 40 to 50 killed and 200 to 250 wounded.

Patrolling activity made the night pretty hectic, but the days were far from uneventful. The decree that men must stand-to at daybreak and nightfall presented a unique opportunity of viewing sunrise and sunset in the trenches. To some the far-flung sunsets flowing over the hills reminded them that they had something more to live for than sleep in a hole in the ground and that comradeship waxes in the nauseous blasphemy of war:

> 'It is strange how unfeeling we are when we are young, how in-sensitive to the plight of others close to us. I often think back with wonder, as one who now has close dealings with boys in their period just before university, to the young soldiers we had in the line then, scarcely older than these and far less travelled (in the

[2] There were few cases of the fearful 'Songo fever' among the British troops in Korea. In the Dukes there was only one – Captain Sam Robertson, who missed the Hook battle because of it. Helicoptered out to a MASH in Seoul he recovered quickly – though not quickly enough for Robertson, who got himself discharged by 'adjusting' the specific gravity of his urine samples.

broader sense of that word). Mine, being assault pioneers, had been sifted from the mining areas for their slight experience with pit props: they had hardly ventured from Durham or South Wales, from the simple societies of heavy labour, when they were confronted with a Korean winter in their late teens. Now they were asked to stand alone or in pairs, in bunkers or open trenches, waiting as the sun set and the gloom brought its attendant crop of half-uttered fears, waiting either for the "stand down" order or for . . . what? Obliteration? I now marvel at their unflinching courage evening after evening as their officers went round the fighting pits checking weapon workings and ammunition supply, telling them that the battle was certainly imminent and that this night might be *the night,* instructing those who carried Sten-guns to fix their bayonets, and passing on to the next pit with a nonchalant smile. I remember noticing that we who moved round the pits (who, though young, knew our soldiering and were perhaps the sons of soldiers) saw well enough that we were among our whole platoon – our gang, our mates, our muckers – all standing tense with apprehension but in a state of solidarity: but they who stood there knew only that Fred was here frightened beside them, and in the next pit there *should be* a couple more and a couple more further on. They stood dogged but isolated in mind, knowing from previous gossip what had happened to two men caught unawares on a standing patrol. And ahead of them was darkness and the enemy. "Like an owl in desolate places, like some lonely bird on a rooftop", as the psalmist said; they waited with patient apprehension which did not grow less as the procedure was repeated the next evening.' [3]

When it was certain that no attack would materialize after the dawn stand-to, the normal business of the day would continue. In their command posts the company commanders would work at the next night's patrolling plan. In the forward platoons sentries would keep watch while such work on the defences as was possible during daylight would continue; the remainder of the defenders would rest and relax. Tea would be brewed, letters

[3] Fr Alberic Stacpoole MC.

would be written, and men would sleep until it was time to stand-to again in the half-light of dusk.

This may appear to be a very domestic picture of life in the front line when an attack was impending, but with an already attenuated battalion spread over a 2000-yard frontage the demands made on the defenders for working parties and patrols meant that no one had very much sleep and everyone was in a state of permanent near exhaustion. In the three weeks before the battle the physical effects of fatigue almost beggar description. Rain compounded the misery:

'Sandbag walls slipped away and trenches tumbled in on themselves, eroded by rain; and with the slide went the phone lines pinned to the walls, some of them lying to be trampled on, while others snapped and broke our communication. To brush against the side of a trench, as we had to do when we passed one another, entailed covering our flanks with clay-mud which the rain then spread over our trousers. And our task was not merely to survive, which was exercise enough, cookers being blown out or food cans filled with rain: our task was still and more than usual "to dominate the enemy". So patrols went on, harassing fire programmes went on, mortar bombs continued to land in our area, and defensive wire continued to be blown down into our trenches. Our task of improving the defensive positions, the daily duty of troops in a static war, became a sort of field first aid, drainage and plumbing. Bunkering and tunnelling ceased for a while as shoring up – with pickets, corrugated iron or mud-filled sandbags – took all our energies.' [4]

Apart from an occasional stonk the Dukes had a quiet day on 19 May. The standing patrols fanned out into positions shortly after 8 pm, and none of them reported anything untoward until 12 minutes before 11 pm. Then all hell broke loose. The first indication that something was about to happen was the racket created by a fight on Warsaw, where one of the standing patrols was obviously in trouble. In Stygian darkness a platoon of

[4] Fr Alberic Stacpoole MC.

Chinese had succeeded in crawling up to a position from which they were able to overwhelm the patrol in a quick rush. The patrol, which had neither time nor opportunity to telephone or send a message over the wireless, fought back with bullets and grenades. The outcome was one man killed, two others wounded and the patrol commander missing. The latter had been knocked on the head and dragged back by the Chinese.

While this fight was going on messages began to flow into the company command posts from other standing patrols. Pieced together it was apparent that there was activity along the whole sector of the Dukes' front; the Chinese were probing the defences.

Bunbury had expected something, since receiving a message from Army Intelligence earlier in the evening. Radio intercepts suggested trouble was afoot although it was not clear whether the expected attack was being mounted.

In the event no attack materialized. But at 11 pm an arabesque of red and crimson Verey lights heralded a crashing barrage. During the next hour and a half more than a thousand shells and mortar bombs fell on the Hook, effectively blotting out any chance of discovering what had happened to the patrol on Warsaw. When a counter-barrage was put up, the continuous drumming of the shells was something to make the hair stand on end. Both sides continued firing until half past midnight, and only then was it possible for men to venture out on the Warsaw ridge. There they found the casualties of the earlier action, very shaken but still holding their position.

By dawn (on the 20th) however, the whole area had quietened down, and Second-Lieutenant David Gilbert-Smith – another of the hard rugger-playing fraternity who was known to the ladies of the regiment as 'Brown Eyes' – took a fighting patrol out to sweep the Warsaw ridge. But there were no Chinese there to sweep. Not that this absence of enemy in daylight meant very much. The sudden flare-up of the night before, combined with the Intelligence warnings, was far more ominous. Après a reconnaissance le déluge was to be expected, and the Dukes grimly got ready for it. At dusk two platoons of the reserve company – Rudolf Austin's 'A' company – moved up to the reverse slope of the Hook.

The curtain of night had barely fallen when it became clear that the precautionary move was likely to be justified. Once again at 11 pm precisely the Chinese were reported to be rampaging about on Warsaw and in larger numbers than ever before. Bunbury was ready for them: the standing patrols were called in and the divisional artillery's barrage smothered the ridge in a cliff of fire. As on the previous night this was countered by a Chinese barrage. Two red flares were seen to shoot up from No Man's Land and five minutes later the first shells and mortar bombs of a fierce concentration fell on the Hook men. It was to last until 2 am, by which time no less than 4,500 projectiles had landed on or around the defences. In a relatively small area this was an unusually high number, and the fact that many of the shells were of 122 mm calibre was of pronounced significance. As was to be expected there were casualties, although the Dukes may be reckoned to be lucky to have escaped with only one killed and nine wounded that night. That was not the complete bill however; the work of re-supply had to continue, and ten Korean porters were also caught in the storm of shells.

Surprisingly enough the heavy 105 mm and 122 mm shells had caused little appreciable damage to the bunkers and weapon pits, and the defenders congratulated themselves. Their defences, they reckoned, would stand up to almost any bombardment. It was an erroneous and unfortunate conclusion which, when the real test came, was seen to be sadly awry.

Again David Gilbert-Smith led a fighting patrol out from the Hook shortly before dawn. This time he was ordered to sweep down Green Finger and to search the caves on its western slopes. As on Warsaw the previous night, the Chinamen had vanished; screams and shots had been heard above the din of the bombardment, so presumably some of them had been laid low. But there was neither sight nor sound of anybody on Green Finger and the caves were empty. Only the fire from a solitary sniper on Seattle indicated that danger still lurked in the offing.

Twenty-first May was almost a repetition of the previous day, except that the focus of the activity that night seemed to be on Ronson, and the patrol on the night of the 22nd was led by Sergeant France. Warsaw, Green Finger, Ronson – would Long Finger be the next avenue of approach to be probed? Sure enough it was.

Before continuing with the sequence, however, it is necessary to recount a number of changes which were to affect the course of the battle. When an attack seemed certain on the night of 20 May, Brigadier Kendrew decided to redeploy his brigade. By dividing the Hook sector into two and bringing another battalion into the line, the Dukes position would be greatly strengthened. This would mean that all three battalions of the 29th Brigade would be in the line. However, General West had promised him the loan of another battalion from the 28th Brigade – which was not then so hard pressed. So a fourth battalion, the 1st Royal Fusiliers entered the lists of the Hook. The redeployment was completed during 23 May, and at the end of it the Dukes remained in occupation of Pt 121, the Hook proper, and the Sausage, with Bunbury's reserve company (still Rudolf Austin's 'A') centrally located behind. The Black Watch took over Pt 146 and deployed an additional company there, with another company behind; their fourth rifle company was sited well behind and between Pt 146 and Sausage in case it was needed for counter-attack in either of the newly formed left or right Hook sectors. The King's, occupying the quiet zone of Yong Dong, remained where they were. But to them fell the task of mounting a diversion which Kendrew hoped might ease the pressure on the Dukes.

For the Black Watch the orders to come out of reserve and get back to the battle came like the douche of cold water which Bertram, their veteran Korean bathboy, was in the habit of sprinkling on officers who visited his establishment. The Jocks were relaxing and regaling 'B' echelon and the supporting troops with gruesome tales of their prowess; David Rose was on his way to relax in Tokyo. Recalled post-haste from Kure, he arrived back to find that Ramsay Bunbury was acting as the Hook supremo, and sixty per cent of the Highlanders were under his command. In the event of a counter-attack it appeared that Rose's task would be to lead his battalion headquarters in a death or glory charge. Mercifully nothing of the sort was required. Joe Kendrew was a wise and capable brigade commander and he realized that the volatile 'Chief' of the Highlanders could be better employed elsewhere. Thus on 27 May the King's vacated Yong Dong and the Black Watch took their place.

Meantime the King's had attempted to stage their diversion. Regrettably it did not turn out to be the success that was hoped for. Kendrew had ordered a night raid on the main Chinese stronghold on Pheasant. This was the centre of activity radiating out to the Hook, and if the Chinese were caught in the middle of No Man's Land forming up for their attack on the Hook he believed that they would be thrown into utter confusion. And, if the diversion had been launched on the night chosen by the Chinese for their assault, they probably would have been put off balance. As it was there was no reliable information on which to work and everything went wrong.

The original intention was for the raid to take place on the night of 23/24 May. But at the eleventh hour it was postponed until the following night. The plan was for three strong fighting patrols found from 'B' Company of the King's to attack Pheasant from a base established shortly after midnight on the near side of the Sami-chon. The company commander, Major Gordon Beard, would hold the base with what was left of his company after the three patrols of one officer and sixteen soldiers each had been formed. From the base, one of the patrols, under command of Second-Lieutenant Haughton, would advance parallel to the river and take up a position to protect the right flank from any Chinese who might approach from the north-east. When Haughton was in position, Second-Lieutenant Caws would take his patrol up the river. Caws would be followed by Second-Lieutenant Ryder's patrol, which would cover Caws's men, while they crossed and subsequently when they returned from their mission. Caws was to carry out the actual assault on Pheasant, under the cover of an artillery and mortar barrage. All three subalterns were young, relatively inexperienced, and National Service men.

Beard's company left their position on Yong Dong a few minutes before midnight on 24 May and set up the base in No Man's Land; Caws's patrol then crossed the river. So far so good; the first two phases of the plan had been accomplished without incident. About 2 am, however, as the patrol was nearing Pheasant, there was a series of explosions and dazzling green flashes. Caws had blundered into an uncharted minefield and ten of his sixteen men were blown up. As so often happens in war, the whole aspect of the operation was changed by the unexpected. With only six unwounded but shaken men, four stretcher cases and six others in varying states of incapacity, the raid had already failed. The only thing to do was to call it off and extricate the wounded. And this was more easily said than done. The artillery boxed in the area with steel and effectively prevented any Chinese interference. But it was a pitch black night and while the darkness had provided a welcome cloak for the raiders, it became a serious impediment during the rescue operation. Ryder's patrol, guarding the river crossing and expecting to fight a rearguard action, had come out heavily armed with Brens and a surfeit of ammunition. Ordered now to cross the river and collect the casualties, their equipment became a liability. Controlling these men floundering about in the Cimmerian gloom was difficult. But the Lancashiremen were as persistent as they were tough. And, although the rescue work took nearly three hours, Beard's exhausted company was back in Yong Dong shortly after 5 am.

On the Hook there was little evidence to show that the Chinese had been distracted by or even concerned about the raid. Indeed, it is possible they were unaware of the difficulties in which the King's found themselves. During the day the Dukes had been subjected to a steady rain of shells, and between 7 pm and 2 am the probing of the Yorkshiremen's positions had continued. On this occasion the Chinese were back where they started a few nights before. Having subjected all the approaches to a general reconnaissance first, they had focused their probes on Warsaw, then on Green Finger and Ronson, and finally on Long Finger. Now they were back on Green Finger.

Where they would concentrate for the attack was the most cogent question after when. If this information was available Bunbury could get his gunners to concentrate their fire on the forming-up places as soon as the full-scale attack was seen to be certain. The pattern of earlier offensives, the activity on Warsaw, and the big caves surreptitiously excavated in the valley below Warsaw seemed to provide a clue. So, on 22 and 23 May, Bunbury decided to investigate these sanctuaries. First on the list were the caves in the re-entrant between Warsaw and Green Finger, and Second-Lieutenant Simon Berry was given the job. Berry, a small, slightly built and gangly individual, with a gay and urbane character, looked the part of the auctioneer he was later to become. Some of his brother officers would not have been surprised if Berry's uniform had been embellished with a bowler hat and neatly rolled umbrella. Behind a casual and flippant manner, however, there was a serious and precise nature, and Berry was a brave and determined young man.

To accompany him on this daring and highly dangerous mission Berry selected Corporal George Stephenson, a level-headed and phlegmatic Yorkshireman. Rudolf Austin, who guarded, guided and watched over the progress of ninety per cent of the Dukes' patrols, was to supervise the mission from a control post on top of the Hook. Radio communication between Berry and Austin would allow the former to report his location and progress, so enabling Austin to direct artillery support when and where it was needed. Throat microphones had gone out of fashion after the Second World War – presumably for some good technical reason. When it came to whispering messages into a radio set in the middle of No Man's Land, at times when Chinamen were suspected, and sometimes known, to be only yards away the lack of such silent-speaking devices was very evident. A crude device improvised from a jam tin which fitted over the speaker's mouth only partially filled the need.

Berry and Stephenson set out from the Hook about 8.45 pm. Their first bound was the standing patrol on Warsaw, which that night was commanded by the belligerent Corporal Mackenzie. Mackenzie, who had managed to get himself out with nearly every fighting and reconnaissance patrol of consequence since the Dukes came to Korea, was highly indignant at not being selected to go on this one. Only a direct order from Austin prevented him from leaving his own patrol and following Berry.

Slipping quietly down into the valley, Berry quickly reached the site of the caves on the eastern slopes of the Warsaw ridge. The first two were unoccupied but fresh scraps of food and other rubbish remained as evidence of recent habitation. Before venturing any farther to explore the others, Berry stopped and radioed this information back to Austin. Barely had the message been passed and acknowledged when a distinctive shuffle and subdued rattle announced the proximity of a party of Chinese behind and to the right of him. A Chinese patrol, twenty strong, was creeping along the edge of Green Finger towards the junction of Sausage and the Hook. Its presence was confirmed five minutes later when Second-Lieutenant Peter Mitchell, a highly strung young man best known for his outstanding qualities on the cricket field, came on the air to report that it had clashed with his standing patrol on Green Finger. Berry, Stephenson and the Chinese had passed each other in the dark without either being aware of the existence of the other. But now that the Chinese were engaged with Mitchell's patrol the immediate danger to Berry was over.

To make sure that he was out of harm's way, however, Austin ordered him to push on out into No Man's Land where he could lay up while a stonk in front of Mitchell's position fixed the troublesome Chinese. When the British barrage crashed down Berry and Stephenson were half-way between their own lines and the Chinese outposts, in a hollow from which they could watch the fireworks over Long Finger and Sausage. (As soon as the British guns fired, the Chinese replied with a stonk on Sausage.)

As time passed and the shelling gave no signs of lifting, Austin deemed it was safe enough for Berry to resume his patrol. So he and Stephenson cautiously made their way back to the northern slopes of Warsaw to begin their exploration of the caves there. The first three they came to were unoccupied and Berry radioed back a report to this effect with his estimate of how many men could shelter in each. At the fourth cave they ran into trouble. Creeping up to the entrance, Berry and Stephenson literally stumbled over three Chinamen. The latter were more surprised than Berry, and two of them tore off into the darkness, while the third dived into the cave. Berry promptly threw a grenade after him, and Stephenson followed it with another when they heard groans. Then, when it seemed reasonably certain that this particular Chinaman had gone to join his ancestors, he and Stephenson went into the cave. A quick search of the body for papers proved fruitless and Berry realized that he and Stephenson would have to get away quickly or risk being caught by other Chinese alerted by the dead man's two companions.

Austin on the Hook had also appreciated what might happen and as soon as Berry came up on the wireless he was ordered to get back into the void of No Man's Land while a plan for his return could be worked out. With the Chinese still milling about around the end of Long Finger, the shortest route was blocked and it was eventually decided that safety depended on a long walk. Thus it was that the two men returned by a circuitous route ending at the Black Watch outposts on Pt 146. Technically as well as physically this was quite an achievement. The short range of Berry's wireless soon put him out of direct contact with Austin and instructions had to be relayed via a radio net which incorporated stations set up by the King's on Yong Dong as well as the Black Watch in Pt 146. In sum this patrol could be judged highly successful. Despite the unforeseen difficulties occasioned by the Chinese, Berry had accomplished everything he was told to do. He had confirmed the existence of prepared sanctuaries in the Long Finger and Warsaw valleys and estimated their capacity. To complete the picture what was needed now was confirmation and estimate of the size of the caves below Green Finger.

This was procured on the night of 24/25 May. At 2 am when the night's activity had simmered down, Corporal Archer and Private Oyston scrambled down the south-east side of Green Finger. The King's raid on Pheasant was in full swing at this time and it was presumed that the Chinese would be busy elsewhere. When the patrol set out neither Archer, Oyston nor Tony Firth, their company commander, knew that Beard's raid was running into difficulties at that very moment. Nor could they have appreciated that the Chinese might be wholly unconcerned about what was happening in front of Pheasant. Fortunately, this was the night they were concentrating their probes on Long Finger and probably the reason why Archer saw and met no enemy. When the patrol returned at 3.30 am Archer had found five caves with tunnel-like entrances, each capable of accommodating twelve men. He and Oyston had heard men moving in the valley at the foot of the spur, but so far as the caves were concerned nobody was in occupation and there were no sentries near them.

With this information the overall pictures seemed to suggest that the Chinese could shelter up to two companies between Warsaw and Long Finger, another company between Warsaw and Green Finger and two platoons, perhaps more, below Green Finger. In the initial stages of an attack the Dukes would need to be prepared for the onslaught of at least one Chinese battalion. If they adhered to their usual tactics this would be followed by at least another battalion, perhaps a third. And for the forward platoons this meant odds of between three and five to one against the Yorkshiremen.

8

MANY ENEMIES, MUCH HONOUR

When the going gets tough, the tough get going.
WEST POINT DICTUM

The escalating concentrations of artillery fire which ravaged the
Hook were intended primarily to harry its garrison and halt
work on the defences. By hammering the forward slopes the
Chinese also hoped to ease the passage of their assault troops
through the tangle of barbed wire which covered all approaches
to the Dukes' weapon pits. Formidable enough in the time of the
Black Watch, the wire fences were now becoming an insur-
mountable obstacle; even trenches and weapon pits had been
roofed in with barbed wire mesh. Bunbury was determined that
the assaulting waves of Chinese infantry would be brought to a
standstill well away from the Dukes' positions, where they
could be dealt with by the guns of the defenders. Responsibility
for carrying out this frantic wiring programme fell to Second-
Lieutenant John Stacpoole.

Tall, slim and good-looking with rather a long face and
straight features, Stacpoole had a quick, clear brain, and a character that was both strong and gentle. Religious, he was tolerant
of the beliefs or disbeliefs of others, and his personality left as
strong an impression on his seniors as it did upon those who
served under him. Devoid of personal ambition, his background and upbringing were those of a true professional. Deep

thinking, he radiated an air of quiet authority vital in the task to which he was committed.

'The Colonel decided that the immediate approaches to the Hook Company should be heavily wired on all sides during the days remaining to us before the expected assault. In consultation with our Sappers, we decided upon a blanket of dannert wire from about thirty yards forward of our fighting bunkers, a continuous fence broken only by patrol routes, stretching 300° around the Hook from in front of "C" Company on the right-rear flank to the Assault Pioneer platoon on the left-rear flank. This blanket, once established by a picket and strand wire fence, could then be thickened up inwards towards the fighting trenches under cover of darkness night after night by shifts; and when we reached our own positions with a veritable forest of wire entanglement, dannert held down by pickets and more dannert coils heaped on top to bring the obstruction to eye height, we decided to go on wiring inwards until most of the Hook looked like a tropical forest of steel undergrowth. The task was given to the Assault Pioneer platoon to do.

It was impossible to wire by daylight or even by very clear moonlight, for Chinese O.P.s and snipers drove us back into our trenches. It was difficult to work out beyond our fighting bays on a still night, for so close were the Chinese O.P.s that they heard our pickets being driven into the ground and could bring approximate directional fire down on to our working parties, using mortars usually and sometimes machine-guns. It was out of the question to use lights above ground, as we were fully exposed on the terrain that at this time was most interesting to the enemy. We had to resort, then, to feeling our way on dark blustery nights, or risking our necks on calm clear nights.

We largely overcame the picket hammering problem with a device the Engineers had already concocted for us, a heavy metal sleeve like a fixed-breech gun barrel, with a solid top to it and a handle on either side, which could be slid over the picket head and run up and down its shaft by two sturdy sappers or assault pioneers, on the ram principle, till the picket was driven far enough into the ground. This was a noisy process until we packed the inside head of the sleeve with sandbags to muffle the strike and put a sandbag over the picket to muffle the sliding action of our two-handled hammer. The process became, after enough practice, swift, accurate and quiet (though never quite silent enough to set our nerves at rest).

Each night's wiring was carefully planned, wiring teams being given exact tasks and an opportunity by evening light to look at the ground they were to grope over, the quartermaster's men delivering exact amounts of field equipment to the best exits as close behind the skyline as possible during the day. We co-ordinated our work programme with outgoing patrols and with repair and building programmes being undertaken by our supporting Sappers (who did not cease reinforcing the fighting bays hit by artillery fire during the previous twenty-four hours). We tried to keep fresh by snatching daylight hours of sleeping, living as we did our most active hours through the night, like troglodites.

The wiring went well, unutterably exhausting as it was; for we had to carry seemingly endless coils of barbed wire, each of them a good weight, up on to the ridge and out on to the ground which by then had been shelled for a couple of years and was full of pitfalls to the blind and weary porter at dead of night. We often stumbled, liable sometimes to fall into our own trenches several feet below with dannert cable crashing on top of us. Our task was disturbed by verey lights, para-illuminating flares and search-lights whenever they suddenly lit up the gloom and caught us moving about on exposed ground – it could be like a rather morbid game of grandmother's footsteps, men being caught in the middle of a tangle of barbed wire unable to do anything but freeze and pretend they were pickets!

We pegged out tracks from the stores area, where the quartermaster's men had left off, out to the night's wiring areas, with white tape and six-inch nails. Ferrying was part of the task, wiring up the other part; and both tasks were done under persistent though often very intermittent harassing fire. As the field of wire grew dense and began to acquire an unmistakable bulk through enemy field glasses morning after morning, the harassing fire grew more regular and better directed night by night, till we became used to expecting four or eight mortar bombs every quarter of an hour dead on the quarter. At about a minute to harassing time we looked for cover either in our trenches or in shell holes, and as soon as the last round of the scheduled shoot had exploded we were on our feet and back at the wiring task: it amused us to be able to pick and play this regularity – the great sin of soldiering is always to become predictable.

One of our main fears when we began the fence in early May was enemy foiling patrols, for we had no cover party apart from one or two of the assault pioneers taking a rest from work. It would not have been difficult for the Chinaman to come close, watch our pattern of work, and at an opportune moment machine-gun those who were pulling out and pinning down dannert coils. But as the fence grew thicker our work area came in close under our own fighting bays and the screen of wire between our working parties and No Man's Land grew more impregnable, till eventually we were wiring inside our own trench perimeter, skylined to shellfire but safe from patrols.' [1]

By the morning of 26 May the wiring programme was well advanced. Virtually everything that could be done for the Hook had been completed during the previous night. Surprisingly enough this night had been remarkably quiet. A two-man 'recce' patrol, which had laid up in the scrub on Green Finger to watch what the Chinese did at first light, had seen nothing. All day the quietude persisted and it was not broken until late that night.

For the Dukes the respite from shelling propitiated a change of the Hook garrison. Brigadier Kendrew, wearing a red-banded helmet and personifying Surtees' Jorrocks, had come to see the Dukes on the 25th, and found 'B' Company 'looking tired'. As officers and men had had precious little sleep in ten days, it is scarcely surprising that Kendrew thought Firth lacked his customary suavity and bounce. A change might be beneficial he suggested to Bunbury. The latter agreed, and 'D' Company on Pt 121 were ordered to swap places with 'B' on the Hook. In an atmosphere of subdued enemy activity this change ran smoothly and Emett got ready to fight a battle which would live in history. [1] Fr Alberic Stacpoole MC.

114

That night the Assault Pioneers tried to finish the wiring programme.

'The night I dreaded came on 26 May, a still evening with a starred heaven, a crystal clear atmosphere and a near-full moon – the kind of night when you can hear dogs bark in the next village and see moving shadows across valleys. "In such a night as this,/ when the sweet wind did gently kiss the trees/ and they did make no noise, in such a night." We went out to continue the wiring programme, but were too closely mortared and eventually had to come in early – it seemed prudent – with half our schedule of work left undone. The next day I telephoned the Colonel to explain this and ask for the right to cancel the next night's programme if the moon and the weather continued like that. The Colonel refused; he said that the wiring was so crucial to the defence programme that he was willing to carry a number of casualties to see it proceed. Until then we had had only one assault pioneer hit by shrapnel, so he spoke with a certain confidence.' [2]

Bunbury's refusal to allow Stacpoole's pioneers to postpone their work in hazardous circumstances revealed a steely purposefulness, which was the greatest single factor contributing to the Dukes' success. It is no light thing to have to issue orders which may send men to their deaths. But in war the need to sacrifice soldiers' lives, if need be, is all too often necessary. The responsibility is a terrible strain, which only the utterly callous can go through and survive without losing years in the process. And Bunbury was not a callous man.

Behind the scenes the Dukes' CO and Major Bill Mackay had been reviewing and revising the tasks of the artillery. How far the gunners can help the infantry basically depends on the numbers of guns and shells available. In this instance there was, fortunately, a sufficiency of both. When the need arose, both the seventy-two 25-pounders of the Commonwealth Division's three field regiments and the Division's heavy mortar battery, would

[2] Fr Alberic Stacpoole MC.

answer the call. U.S. Marine and Turkish field regiments, plus a U.S. battery of 8-inch 'Persuaders' were all incorporated into a comprehensive and awesome catalogue of D.F. and D.F. (S.O.S.) tasks covering every inch of the terrain in front of the Dukes' positions. One D.F. task went even further. When the code word 'Iron Ring' was passed back to the gunners, the 25-pounders would blast the Hook defences themselves. Men would be safe in the bunkers and tunnels, but the hail of proximity fused shell would cut men to pieces above ground.

Adjusting the existing plans, deciding what ground should be covered, what concentration of fire would suffice, and for how long, was a laborious process, akin to arranging the score for a symphonic poem. The terrain with its defensive overlay and avenues of approach open to the Chinese constituted the burden of the piece; the guns, the mortars, the supporting tanks and the Dukes' own flat trajectory small arms were the instruments; and the form of the music had to be flexible enough to cater for variations introduced by the Chinese. There was no shortage of ammunition, but there was the need to conserve resources to cater for attacks at other places at other times. Bunbury, a keen racing man, was accustomed to making rapid assessments of changing odds, and his computing was often completed before Mackay had finished setting his slide-rule.

On the afternoon of 26 May the gunners ranged in the 'Persuaders'. With field artillery this 'ranging' procedure was a simple business. Infantry in the forward positions were warned of what was to happen and told to remain under cover while the shoot was conducted. But on this late afternoon Emett's men were pulled back behind the crest of the Hook. One Persuader fired only one shell per minute, but each of these shells contained 200 pounds of high explosive and none of the Dukes' bunkers would have stood up to a shortfall of this power. In the circumstances prevailing on the afternoon of 26 May, the risk of leaving the forward defences unattended was considered to be less than the risk of devastation from one of the 8-inch shells.

'We watched entranced, as the whole ground trembled. It was not so much like artillery fire, I remember thinking, as like depth charges being allowed to sink deep into the water before they blew up, setting up shock waves all around them. The warning sound of their fly-in seemed to come from farther away and higher up than was so with 25-pounders, and there was a sense of magnitude and magnificence at impact. They perfectly answered the American love of the grandiose.'[3]

By 10.30 pm that night it appeared that the Chinese had also acquired a sense of the grandiose. Perhaps they were merely responding to the ominous performance of the afternoon with a tone-poem of their own. For an hour and a half the Hook, the Sausage and Pt 121 were plastered with shells and mortar bombs.

Before the bombardment started John Stacpoole had taken his Assault pioneers out to finish their tasks:

'The night (of 27 May) proved to be another idyllic scene of pastoral bliss, another danger trap to those who need darkness for their work. We had two pockets of wiring to complete in the two parts of the night, one in the hollow between the Hook Company and "C" Company, the other immediately forward of the Hook point fighting bunkers. These we began with more than usual nervousness: I remember a particular foreboding that night, feeling that our luck had held too long.

About five minutes before we had completed our "C" Company task, two mortar bombs whistled in on top of us. I was thrown off my feet, as if punched in the back and face together, and found myself lying on the ground some yards away, bleeding from the jaw and with a largish lump of shrapnel stuck in the small of my back up against the backbone. Four of my pioneers also had pieces of shrapnel in their legs or thighs – none, mercifully, in a serious way. I remained on the ground watching while the job was completed, and then we took ourselves – like rugger crocks back to the pavilion – back to Hook Company HQ, where I reported the state of the game and then fainted from delayed shock.

[3] Fr Alberic Stacpoole MC.

Another officer tried to take a reassembled team of assault pioneers out on to the front of the Hook that night, but they were almost immediately blown off by harassing fire in the now uncannily good visibility. That was the last of the wiring done: the next night our work was to be thoroughly tested.'[4]

Frivolous reference to 'rugger crocks' disguises the seriousness of the wound which Stacpoole sustained. Limping into Emett's command post, the first person he encountered was Rudolf Austin. 'Good evening, Rudolf, Sir,' he announced, 'I've just been wounded.' 'Where?' 'In the back, I think.' 'Trousers down . . . My God!' Austin winced when he saw the steel splinter protruding from the small of Stacpoole's back which had been rubbing against his spine. Then it was that Stacpoole fainted; for him the battle was over.

> 'I remember the casualty evacuation process well. I was revived with whisky on the floor of the HQ bunker, a blanket around me. We joked about "iron in your bum" and "spoiled good looks". A stretcher jeep was called up and motored me back to Ernest Mackie at the RAP, who made disenchanted noises about the smallness of the wound, albeit against the backbone, and fiddled with the protruding metal. I next found myself in a MASH feeling sick and gave my exhausted body to many hours' sleep. When I woke up, I found around me numbers of wounded Dukes talking about the battle, and I realized that I had missed the main match by twenty-four hours.'[4]

At the 'D' Company command post, Emett was worried that the barrage which prevented the Assault Pioneers from completing their wiring programme heralded the long-overdue attack. But apart from seeing a platoon of Chinamen on Ronson, who ran back to Seattle when the guns were called in, nothing happened that night. But the next morning, when it was possible to make a coherent assessment, the latest bombardment assumed a new significance. Of the 166 shells which had been counted,

[4] Fr Alberic Stacpoole MC.

the greater proportion were of 105 and 122 mm calibre; more heavy guns had been dug in and registered.

There was no return to the lull of the previous day. Shelling and mortaring began at 5.30 am and continued intermittently throughout the day, 400 rounds falling on the Hook and 15 on Sausage. Some were bound to reach their mark and as the inevitable stream of casualties flowed into the regimental aid post, Ernest Mackie and his RAMC assistant, the stocky Sergeant Sandy Powell, were kept busy. At dusk the standing patrol moving into position on Ronson suffered a direct hit. It is a terrible thing for a body of living men to be hit naked in the open by a shell. All life ceases at once, or ebbs away in gulps on to the ground around. The shape of the human form gives place to tangled fibres and butchered flesh. The shock it causes to on-lookers will drain them of all vitality. On this occasion the patrol suffered such severe casualties – four killed and three wounded – that it was virtually wiped out. Replacements were found by 'A' Company, but this patrol and the ones on Green Finger had twice to be called in while the gunners shot D.F. tasks over Green Finger. Meantime the Chinese were also shooting, and it was obvious when they scored direct hits on both the Green Finger and Warsaw patrols that they had accurately pinpointed the locations of the outposts.[5] This did not augur well for the future.

Out in No Man's Land another drama was unfolding as Captain Colin Glen and Corporal Duncan Taylor moved cautiously towards a preselected listening post. The two men had spent a week studying the ground from a vantage point on Sausage and preparing for their mission. When it seemed that preparations for the attack had reached a crucial stage – as was now the case – Glen and Taylor would trigger the ultimate alert. Judging by the work that had been done on the caves the pattern of the Chinese attack was clear. Under cover of dark-

[5] The Green Finger patrol suffered one casualty, that on Warsaw four – of which one was fatal.

ness and an artillery barrage their assault troops would cross No Man's Land and form up in the shelter of the caves. At the most it would be only a matter of an hour before they swarmed up Warsaw, Green Finger and Ronson to rush the Hook. If in this brief interval the Dukes could be alerted they would start the battle at an advantage.

Both Glen and Taylor had volunteered for the job; the two unfortunately were not entirely compatible. Colin Glen, a highly strung and gauntly handsome South African, had acquired as Bunbury's adjutant a touch of arrogance ill befitting a young officer of his experience. Zealous and painstaking he had fitted in well until he blotted his copybook for staying out one night during the Commonwealth Division training period; he had discovered a girl friend with a concert party and a visit to renew his acquaintance, understandably if not permissively, was unduly prolonged. When Hugh LeMesurier took over the adjutancy Glen became the Dukes' 'patrol master', responsible for co-ordinating the activities of the Dukes' patrols with the gunners and the battalions on either side of the Hook. 'Spud' Taylor, formerly a regular soldier with the West Yorkshire Regiment, had been on the reserve when he was recalled. Having been in Burma and fought with the West Yorkshires through the bloody battles for Kohima, he applied to join the Dukes, hoping that active service would bring promotion. Thirty years old, stocky, weather-beaten and resourceful, without his uniform Taylor could have fitted into the mining background of Doncaster or the steelworks of Sheffield. Indeed military environment appeared to have singularly little effect on his nature and outlook. He was typical of the British soldier of all ages in history, without doubt his double would have been present in the Peninsula or on the Marne.

The decision to send out the patrol was taken on the morning of 26 May, and Glen and Taylor set out from the 'V' Company sector on Pt 146 in the deepening dusk that night. The Jocks, who were to be relieved next day by the King's wished them luck when they climbed out of the communication trench and scrambled through the wire. The two men had enough food and water to see them through the next forty-eight hours, and each carried an 88 wireless set beside a Sten and a stock of grenades. Taylor had greased and prepared his Sten with loving care – fitting double springs into each of the magazines to increase the cyclic rate of fire, and taping magazines together in opposing pairs to speed up reloading. Glen carried benzedrine tablets to ward off sleep and morphine injectors for emergency.[6]

In the eerie half-world of cold blackness and menace under the curving roof of shells, the patrol's destination was a solitary bush about a mile below Green Finger. From air photographs and their observations on Sausage and the Hook this bush stood between tracks criss-crossing the valley between the Chinese lines and the lower slopes of the Hook. The ground nearby was uneven and with luck they could hide in some hollow from which they could keep tabs on the Chinese and radio their findings back to the Hook; from there Rudolf Austin would relay their news to the Battalion Command Post.

In the darkness the journey out to the bush was probably the most difficult part of the operation. Finding it would not be easy either, but once they were there it was reasonable to suppose that they would escape detection unless a Chinaman actually stumbled over them. Walking slowly along a well-worn path past the minefields at the bottom of Long Finger they moved well out into the middle of No Man's Land. Shells and mortar bombs whirred overhead to crash on the Hook; every now and then a flare would force them to freeze; periodically the searchlights of the Centurions would shimmer over the ridges and give Glen a chance to verify his bearings. From the direction of

[6] Until the Dukes came to the Hook most of the junior officers had carried morphine. Using it when a doctor is not available to ease a wounded man's pain seems a simple humanitarian act. But it is one that can hazard the life of the individual concerned and Ernest Mackie had asked for the morphine to be withdrawn.

Warsaw a jabbering of voices and the dull thud of picks on rocky soil denoted the presence of men working on the caves. Twice they were compelled to stop and seek cover while squads of Chinese trotted past, heading towards the Hook. Contrary to popular belief, Taylor's impression was that the Chinese were noisy and that they moved in disorganized formations, urged on by commanders who led from the rear.

Eventually they reached a track running at right angles to their path. This was the route they had been seeking, the approach to their objective. Navigation after that was easy and both men were free to concentrate on what was the real business of their mission. Once arrived at the bush they were able to relax. In the misery of finding one's way it is easy almost to forget about what is to happen when you get there. Getting there at all becomes an obsession, not what happens after arrival.

The first thing to do was to report their initial accomplishment. And it was then that Glen's radio was found to be out of order; lucky, therefore, that they had duplicated their means of communication.

Throughout the next day Glen and Taylor lay huddled in a shallow depression about a mile from Emett's outposts. There was little evidence of the Dukes, but men in padded clothes could be seen moving about on Seattle, though it was impossible to see just what they were doing. The day passed slowly, and Glen, afraid of dozing, swallowed too many benzedrine tablets for Taylor's liking. Every two hours they radioed back to the Hook; most of the reports were a simple 'Nan Tare Roger' (Nothing To Report).

Nightfall brought a fresh flush of Chinese activity and an increase of tension. Parties of men trotted past on their way to or coming back from the Hook throughout the night. Some passed within a few yards of the patrol's hideout while Glen and Taylor crouched back, fingers curling round triggers and grenades laid ready to throw. In such circumstances all human sounds heighten the tension; the fewer noises that can be heard the better. In a way the whine of shells, the crash of mortar bombs and the rattle of small-arms fire are comforting sounds because they cannot be mistaken. In the uncompromising dark of No Man's Land it is a brave man who is not paralysed by fear.

It was now 28 May. On the Hook the mortaring and shelling started again about 10.15 am and it did not stop until the long awaited battle was over. The Chinese had completed their preparations and the full fury of their artillery was turned on to the Hook. Shortly before 2 am heavy guns started to pick off individual weapon pits and dug-outs.

One of the two Centurions dug into the Hook was hit and although the tank remained in action, Lieutenant George Forte was wounded. (Forte, a Yorkshireman whose family had regimental ties with the Dukes, was evacuated and helicoptered back to hospital.)

Routine was forgotten as bunkers collapsed and men were buried alive. On the right half of 'D' Company's forward sector, the platoon headquarter bunker received four directs in quick succession and the occupants were entombed. Two hours elapsed before they could be extricated. Nine casualties included two of the three section commanders. Sandhurst-trained Second-Lieutenant Edward Dasent was severely shaken. Partially blinded by a stone, he hurried to Emett's command post to report that his position was 'becoming untenable'. 'Balls,' said Emett curtly, 'get back!'

At this moment Emett would probably have welcomed the arrival of a screaming mob of Chinese. But it was still not certain whether this unprecedented bombardment was the preliminary to an infantry assault. All that was certain was that the Chinese were taking more pains to smash the defences than ever before. Following the punishment meted out to Dasent's platoon the Chinese turned their attentions to other targets. On the crest of the Hook two of the five occupants of a Browning machine-gun post covering approaches to the summit were killed and the remaining three wounded when a shell slammed straight into its embrasure. Weapon pits and fire bays of the left platoon, opposing the crucial approaches from Ronson and Green Finger, were badly damaged, and some of the communication trenches were almost obliterated. In the skies an Auster aircraft, scudding up and down the valley trying to pinpoint the Chinese guns, found itself in the middle of an anti-aircraft barrage the like of which had rarely been encountered in Korea.

At 4 o'clock in the afternoon Bunbury went up to the Hook to see the situation for himself. With shells cascading down and great gaps in the communication system already apparent the outlook was grim. But despite the severity of the bombardment, he was not yet convinced that the Chinese would launch an all-out attack. Up to now all that had happened after previous bombardments was a flush of what might be described as vigorous patrol activity; perhaps this was just the foreplay to another probe. When the Chinese concentrated for an attack some warning could be expected; their radio chatter ought to provide the first clue, and Glen in No Man's Land could be expected to signal more positive warning when the attack got under way. But the radio interceptors had so far not reported any undue traffic in the Dukes' sector and Glen had not expressed any alarm. For the moment, therefore, the most pressing need was to repair the damage that had been wrought and a plan was worked out with Emett for doing this after dark. RE sappers and Stacpoole's weary Pioneers would come up to the Hook during stand-to and help the garrison to reinstate the trenches and battered weapon pits.

A little over two hours later the situation had deteriorated, and it began to look as if something considerably more than a mere probe would be staged that night. At 6 pm the Ronson standing patrol was again caught by a blast of mortar bombs while moving up the communication trench to take up its position. With one man killed and five seriously wounded, the patrol was for the second time in 48 hours virtually obliterated, and after what was left of it had been evacuated to hospital and mortuary a replacement had to be detailed and organized. (By the time this had been done, it was too late, and the patrol joined Emett's reserve platoon.) News that Chinese wireless messages were crowding the ether with chatter came next and Army Intelligence told Brigadier Kendrew that an attack on the Hook was on its way.

Picking up the telephone, Bunbury spoke to Emett. 'Baron,' he said, '*Tonight* is the Night. Cancel the plans for the working parties.' He then went on to explain the details of the last-minute deployments he had ordered. Two platoons of 'A' Company would move up to the Hook, as reserves for use in counterattacks; they would remain behind the crest until needed. 'A' Company's third platoon would be split up: One section would reinforce Dasent's platoon and replacing the casualties of the afternoon bring it up to strength; the platoon commander, John Keatley, and his platoon headquarters, would reinforce and take over command of Stacpoole's Assault Pioneers, deployed in the saddle between the Hook and Pt 121; men of the third section would be used as guides if the situation got to the stage when more reinforcements were needed on the Hook. This effectively disposed of 'A' Company and left Bunbury without any immediate reserves. So Beard's company of the King's would move into the positions vacated by Rudo''
Austin's men.

By 7.45 pm the re-shuffle was completed and everybody was in position. Just in time. As the shelling rose to a new fury Emett spoke to his platoon and section commanders over the radio link – 'Enemy attack imminent. STAND FAST.'

9

THE THIRD BATTLE FOR THE HOOK

The battle began in fading light and faint drizzle. At 7.50 pm
the bombardment suddenly rose to a new crescendo on the
Hook, and faded equally sharply three minutes later. Then
came the attack. Following close on the heels of the barrage
Chinese Infantry, with Assault Engineers carrying pole charges
and petrol bombs, swarmed up Green Finger. Two minutes
later they were on top of the forward positions. A gunner manning an observation post a few yards behind the forward position
on the left came on the air, reporting excitedly that Chinese were
clambering over the trenches in front of him. The message
ceased abruptly in the middle of a sentence, and the gunner's
body was found next morning beside the wreckage of his radio.

In No Man's Land, Glen and Taylor were also able to send
one final message on their remaining radio set. 'This is it!' said
Glen, before their second radio faded out for ever. With
Chinese platoons racing past their hideout he and Taylor
could do nothing but watch and wait. They had intended to
return when darkness fell but this was impossible now. Directly
in front of them a fierce battle was developing and to attempt

moving laterally across No Man's Land would mean crossing the path of oncoming Chinese formations. Out of communication and unable to move, Glen and Taylor were committed to lonely hibernation until the battle was decided.

A mile away, in one of the forward positions about to be overrun, Major Lewis Kershaw was manning the wireless intended to control Glen and Taylor's destiny. Kershaw, whose normal duties kept him back in 'B' echelon, had taken Austin's place as their rear link. Austin had been out on the Hook for five nights in succession supervising and co-ordinating the Dukes' patrols, and that morning Bunbury had ordered him to get some sleep. 'Kershaw will take over tonight,' he had said. And Kershaw was happy to do so. If there was any snag in the arrangement, it was that he and Emett did not get on very well together. When it came to the crunch the Baron meant to fight the battle with a minimum of interference and Kershaw was senior to him. 'You can't work here,' he snapped when Kershaw appeared at 'D' Company's command post. 'You'd better find somewhere with one of the forward platoons.' Kershaw had not argued; communication with Glen might be easier if he did go forward. So he had humped his radio up to 10 Platoon's headquarters dug-out. There his presence was welcomed by the platoon commander, Second-Lieutenant Ernest Kirk. Quiet, unassuming and easy-going, Kirk was a National Service man, twenty-one years and three weeks old. As he was due to be demobilized in a matter of weeks he was confident that this would be his last battle – as indeed it was. And he looked forward to the experience of winning.

When the Chinese charged up the Green Finger ridge Kershaw was with Kirk in the latter's platoon headquarters dug-out. One of the tunnels dug by the Black Watch connected it with an observation post in the forward communication trench and it was in this tunnel that Kirk, Kershaw and the men with them took shelter. When three direct hits by heavy shells struck the platoon bunker in quick succession Kersaw ordered everybody back into the tunnel. The earth was shaking, the din was indescribable and from what he could see outside a mammoth plough seemed to be chewing the hillside. To stay in the bunker would have been suicidal, and without point; better, he decided, to get under cover until the shelling slackened.

The forward trenches now no longer existed as such and few of the men who had been caught in them during the barrage were in a fit state to resist the screaming mob of Chinese pouring up the slopes. There was no time to send a message to say what was happening with wireless sets smashed and buried and telephone cables chopped and cut; there was no quick means of doing so anyway.

The tunnel in which Kershaw's party had taken shelter was attacked from both ends simultaneously and Kirk at the platoon headquarter end was the first casualty. Having evacuated his command post his prime concern was to re-establish communication with Emett. Unfortunately the wireless head-set was missing, buried somewhere among the debris in the bunker; going back to search for it, he was cut down by a burst of Burp gun fire. Glimmering torches carried by the Chinese exposed them to the men in the tunnel, and Kershaw brought his Sten into action. Screams, hysterical yells, and shouted gibberish then punctuated an interchange of automatic fire and the dull thump of mortar bombs on the hillsides beyond this microcosm of battle. Wounded in the foot, Kershaw hurled grenades and shouted defiance at the attackers, and the Chinese replied in like measure, until they sickened of the fight, hurled a petrol bomb at the defenders, and blew in the entrance.

Blocked at one end, the fight for the tunnel continued at its other mouth. Corporal George Pickersgill was at this entrance when four or five Chinese bore down on him, firing as they came. He returned their fire and forced the Chinese back. But they were reinforced almost immediately and came back into the tunnel shining torches and throwing grenades. Pickersgill drew back into the tunnel to continue the fight until he was hit by a grenade. Severely wounded and hardly able to see through the blood streaming from his face, he kept shooting at the Chinese even then – until they withdrew and blew in this remaining entrance to the tunnel.

Sealed like in a tomb ten men remained alive in the depths. 'It was Hell in a four-and-a-half-foot hole,' said one of them later. But for Lewis Kershaw one or two might have gone mad. Badly hurt and suffering from the loss of blood, it was his undaunted spirit which held the survivors together. 'The Dukes don't die,' he shouted, 'stick it.' And they did stick it. When dawn broke on the morning of 29 May rescue parties broke into the tunnel and Kershaw was still in command. 'See that I am the last out,' he said. Only then did he lapse into unconsciousness.

Corporal John Walker's section sought refuge in another tunnel when the attack started. Walker himself fought the Chinese back from one of its two entrances while a barricade of bedding was built. When the Chinese threw in satchel charges the tunnel was blocked and Walker's men were left gasping for air. Meanwhile another fight was going on at the other entrance, where Privates Smith and Weallens were desperately trying to hold off more Chinese. When the two Yorkshiremen were wounded they swept forward and at the blocked end of the tunnel the men with Walker heard one of the Chinese ask in English, 'Where are your friends?' and Smith, who had been wounded in both legs, was heard to reply, 'Not in this tunnel'. The voice of Weallens, who was apparently retreating up the tunnel, was then heard to say, 'There's no more up here', before he turned back to his captors. At this Walker moved cautiously up the tunnel, and fired when he saw torches approaching. Screams indicated that some of his bullets had found their mark and the Chinese must have turned back. Then came the inevitable explosion which sealed the tunnel. Like the men with Kershaw the survivors of Walker's section were entombed until the morning. 'We were in darkness and choking through dust and lack of air. One chap alone had half a bottle of water and he shared it all round, all getting a lick every hour.'

Although men were still fighting in the tunnels, the Chinese gained a foothold on the Hook within minutes of the start of the attack. The situation in Dasent's platoon area was only marginally less desperate, as the assault up Green Finger was followed by another, and another and yet another. While the first attackers tried to mop up Kirk's platoon area, fresh waves of Chinamen raced along Ronson, circled round and broke on what remained of the wire in front of Dasent's position. There their impetus was slowed by the devastation as much as the wire, and they were decimated by a holocaust of air burst shells and small-arms fire. Every gun and mortar which could be brought to bear on the approaches to the Hook was now projecting its lethal missiles as fast as men could load. Belts rattled through Sam Robertson's machine guns; the Black Watch were firing across the front from Yong Dong while the Turks were doing the same on the other side.

The decision to initiate this holocaust was taken at 8.25 pm. Ten minutes before this Emett had asked for everything the gunners could give. But Bunbury had hesitated. Glen and Taylor were still in No Man's Land, and as there had been no word from them they might well be trying to crawl back to the Dukes' lines. Asking the artillery to blast Green Finger and the routes along which the Chinese were expected to cross No Man's Land was thus tantamount to signing their death warrant. It was a cruel decision to have to make. During the months they had worked together Bunbury had become attached to his ex-adjutant, and this made the decision even more poignant. One of the worst features of war is that the need to sacrifice men's lives all too often becomes a matter of opting for the least costly alternative. In this instance, however, Bunbury endeavoured to strike a compromise. Hoping that Glen's radio might still be able to receive even if it were unable to transmit, he ordered his signal officer to send a message to the effect that he and

Taylor had five minutes to get away from the danger zone. To help them to do so, the artillery would fire five minutes smoke . . . then the holocaust would be unleashed.

With both their radios completely out of action Glen and Taylor were incapable of receiving any message. And at that moment they were struggling across No Man's Land. After some argument about whether they should stay where they were, attempt to negotiate the direct route back to the Dukes' lines up Green Finger or take a wide sweep round to Pt. 146, they had decided that the latter course would be best. Shells were falling on Pt 146 and Glen was chary about their reception by men of the King's, whose trigger-happiness would have been provoked by the battle raging on the Hook. Yet an attempt to walk back through the middle of a battle was clearly suicidal, and to stay where they were until daylight scarcely less dangerous. So they had set off towards Pt 146.

Colin Glen was leading the way down a track when, perhaps an hour later, a violent explosion knocked both men off their feet. The valley they were traversing was sown with mines and it is possible that Glen had stepped on to one. Judging by Taylor's own injuries and his account of those sustained by Glen, the probability is that a stray shell was the cause. Taylor came to lying a few yards from Glen's body, and when he was able to crawl over it was obvious that Glen was dead. Bleeding from multiple wounds, dazed and shocked, Taylor threw off his combat jacket and staggered on. Every few minutes he would fall to the ground unconscious. Sheer grit saw him through the rest of the night until at 5 am he passed out for the last time 300 yards in front of the Kings' positions.

When the attack was launched in Kirk's position Second-Lieutenant Geoffrey Ingram found himself in the same predicament as Emett's other two platoon commanders. Until the shelling concentrated on 'D' Company's area lifted, Ingram's men were unable to raise their heads above the parapet; his radio was out of action, some of his platoon's weapon pits had been blasted out of existence, and a long stretch of the communication trench to Kirk's position had collapsed. Dust obscured his view, but from the screams and rattle of small-arms fire it was evident that a life and death struggle was in progress less than 200 yards away. In a matter of minutes the Chinese might well be on top of Ingram's positions. Sure enough, as Sergeant Simpson, the platoon sergeant, posted men to block their approach, Chinamen were racing up to the wire. Twelve were counted in the first wave; behind them another thirty followed in open order. Most of them were toppled when Ingram's Brens opened up; a well-thrown enemy grenade knocked out one of the Brens but its crew joined the other gun to fill magazines and keep it in action. On the other side of the platoon locality, the men of Ingram's third section were shooting madly at Chinese they could see on Ronson. They were joined by four men of 'A' Company sent up to replace the patrol annihilated on its way out to Ronson. One of these men, Private Wilfred Husband, threw a grenade which stopped one lot of Chinamen. But others came on shouting to the Dukes 'Surrender!' Working their way round Husband's little party, the Chinamen climbed on to the roof of Husband's weapon pit and were trying to lob grenades into it when Husband cut them down. But a few minutes later a mortar bomb landed outside the dug-out blowing it in and imprisoning the occupants until the morning. Meantime Emett had ordered everybody outside in Ingram's area to take cover before the artillery curtain shifted back and thundered down on their heads. It was now 8.30 pm.

In 'D' Company's command post the occupants were trying to pierce the metaphorical fog of war. Behind the smoke-blackened entrance curtain the dug-out was filled to overflowing. Two signallers, a couple of orderlies, Captain John Gordon, the gunner FOO, Captain Tony Sherratt, the second-in-command, a spare subaltern, Lieutenant Jim Newton, two tables and the usual hotch-potch of equipment and personal kit, and of course, Emett, were all crammed in this tiny bunker. Smoke,

an incessant chatter from the two wirelesses and the reverbera-
tions of the noise outside all contributed to the Journey's End
atmosphere, in which Emett's dominating personality provided
the focal point. 'Watch the door,' he told Sherratt sharply, 'they
could be here any minute.' One of the signallers interrupted him.
'The CO wants you on the set.' Emett turned back and a brief
radio altercation followed. Bunbury wanted to know what was
going on; Emett had no clear idea. Emett should find out and
report back; Emett wanted Battalion Headquarters to stop
pestering him.

The occupants of the battalion command post were clamouring for information. The rare sight of shells dropping behind the
Hook in the paddy fields less than fifty yards away had been the
first out-of-the-ordinary signs that something was brewing up.
When the whole of the top of the Hook was seen to be cased in
steel it was obvious that the long-awaited battle had started.
From Sausage and Pt 121 Kavanagh and Firth reported that
they were subjected to the heaviest artillery concentration they
had ever known. 'Nobody could leave their dug-outs,' said
Kavanagh. 'If you wanted to pee, you just had to stand at the
door, taking great care of course!' In the excitement nobody
thought to tell Ernest Mackie to prepare for a flood of casualties.
Until the middle of the night, when the ferocity of the bombardment eased, none of those wounded on the front slopes of the
Hook could be evacuated to the regimental aid post. But behind
the crest of the hill men waiting to go into battle were struck
by flying splinters and an increasing number of wounded began
to occupy Mackie's attention. In his first lull, occasioned by a
fresh spurt of Chinese shelling on the hilltops, the doctor walked
across to the battalion command post and addressed himself to
Hugh LeMesurier. 'Can someone tell me,' he asked, 'what's
going on up there?'

By this time it was clear that the battle was in full swing 'up
there', and the battalion headquarters staff were immersed in
their separate responsibilities. At one end of the dug-out

LeMesurier, sitting in front of a conglomeration of wireless sets and field telephones, functioned as stage manager. Major Bob Moran, Bunbury's Second-in-Command who, according to the manual dictating the code for conduct of a battle, should have been miles away at the rear of echelon headquarters, 'Left Out of Battle' but ready to take over if Bunbury became a casualty, nervously paced up and down the restricted confines of the command post, smoking the cigarettes of those who had come to tolerate his cheery habit of cadging. Gary Hall, the orderly room regimental quartermaster sergeant, was not actually in the command post but he presided over the battalion rolls in a nearby bunker. Like Moran, Hall was also slated as an 'LOB', but his presence that night was invaluable when it came to the prompt preparation of 'Notices' – the record of casualties that terminated in the dreaded telegram, 'Her Majesty the Queen regrets to inform you that . . .'

Communication between the forward companies and the battalion command post was restricted to wireless throughout the night. Within minutes of the battle starting, the ten-line cable snake to the forward areas had been severed in dozens of places, and repairs were not effected until the following morning. But within their limitations the radios worked well. 31-sets linked Bunbury to his company commanders; and beyond the company command posts the platoons were served by 88-sets. In anticipation of special problems on the Hook, a spare wireless set was set up in a latrine below Emett's command post. The theory was that if all else failed someone from Emett's company headquarters could dash down to the latrine and pass a message on the set conveniently placed above the thunder box. In the event this scheme never worked. The radio was pre-set and only needed to be switched on, but an excited signaller spun the controls and a golden opportunity for passing authentic latrinograms was lost.

In modern war battles are largely decided by the efficiency of communications, since commanders at all levels depend on getting information on which to base their decisions. (In this instance, the gunners were able to switch the devastating power of the Commonwealth artillery from one threatened area to another because Bunbury's information enabled him to anticipate the attacks.) To supplement his sources of information early in the battle, Bunbury turned to Rudolf Austin. The latter, it will be recalled, had been ordered to bed: his place as a controller of the Glen–Taylor patrol having been taken by Lewis Kershaw. Roused from sleep when the battle began, Austin took his company headquarters up to the Hook, to a place behind the crest and just beyond the steel curtain from where he could watch the progress of the battle. From this location he was able to talk to Emett, to listen to the wireless conversation of the latter's platoon commanders, and relay information back to Bunbury.

While Bunbury was pressing for information, Emett was frantically trying to sort out the situation on the Hook. With no word from either of his forward platoons, it looked as if the forward slopes were in enemy hands and only Ingram's depleted platoon stood between the Chinese and his command post. 'Go and see what's going on,' he said to Sherratt, who was still standing by the entrance. Sherratt stepped out into the communication trench, illuminated by an eerie glow compounded of reflected searchlight, star shells and flares. Turning right at the first junction he set off towards Dasent's platoon, ducking whenever a shell landed near. He had not gone very far when the trench terminated in a heap of rubble. Negotiating this would mean climbing out of the trench to the open ground which was being swept by a steady stream of steel splinters. So, turning back, he tried to reach Kirk's platoon; again he was stopped by a fall in the communication trench, where three ashen-faced soldiers were shooting in the direction he was headed. 'You won't get far up there!' said one. So Sherratt stumbled back to Emett. 'Go and organize a counter-attack,' Emett now ordered. Sherratt was nonplussed as well as scared. Counter-attack what, with

whom? 'Collect all the men you can find round here and organize *something*,' said Emett.

Sherratt ventured out again. Apart from those who were in
the command post, only a few of the individuals constituting
company headquarters remained up the hill; all the administrative staff were with 'B' echelon – where Sherratt himself would
have been if the battle had not caught him in the forward area. At
the nearest bunker to the command post he was met by a be-
spectacled gunner; three other men were collected from a second
bunker. For a counter-attack force they were not exactly an
imposing team, so Sherratt told them to stand by and continued
down the trench. He knew that Bunbury had ordered at least
one platoon of 'A' Company up to the Hook and they could not
be very far away.

At 8.45 pm the Chinese launched a second attack on the
Hook. Fresh troops advanced up Warsaw and although they
were badly savaged by artillery, tank and machine-gun fire, they
succeeded in joining hands with the survivors of the first attack.
Fierce hand-to-hand fighting broke out and Dasent's men were
steadily forced back to a line barely thirty yards from Emett's
command post.

At that particular moment Emett did not realize how close
the enemy had penetrated. Dasent's radio did not respond to
his requests for information, and in sheer desperation he ordered
one of his signallers to 'get out there, and either get the bloody
wireless working or fix up the telephone'. Edwin Davies, the
signaller concerned, was a Welshman from Cardiff and known
by his friends as 'Happy Baby'. He did not exactly relish his
assignment. But he set off up the trench traversed earlier by
Sherratt. Where it petered out he ran slap into two Chinamen.
'Come with me,' said one in broken English, seizing the Welshman's arm. 'Not bloody likely,' replied 'Happy Baby', as he
kicked and punched his way out of their grasp. Seizing both of
their Burp guns, he ran back to the command post to blurt out

his story. Further evidence that the Chinese were too close for Emett's liking came subsequently from one of Ingram's men who had allowed three men to squeeze past him in the trench before he realized they were Chinese.

Sudden clarification of the situation came at 9 pm when a radio message reported from Dasent's area, 'Platoon split into three groups. One mortared, two casualties. Second group driven back by shellfire. Third group engaged enemy bunker clearing party, two wounded. All parties attempting to retake fighting bunkers.' A young lance-corporal had recovered the wireless which had accompanied the Ronson patrol, and got it working. And, although his report proved to be slightly optimistic, it was certainly encouraging.

Action to correct and stabilize the situation on the Hook was in fact now under way. Responding to Emett's repeated demands for reinforcements, Bunbury had ordered Tony Firth to send a platoon from Pt 121 up to the Hook. The task was assigned to Scotland's rugger wing forward David Gilbert-Smith. To replace him on Pt 121 one of Beard's platoons was ordered forward. Following a hair-raising ride in Oxford carriers along a heavily shelled road, Second-Lieutenant Michael Ryder and his Kingsmen joined Firth, to arrive at the start of a new phase of the battle.

As Ryder's men deployed, two fresh companies of Chinese attacked Pt 121. But the approaches to Firth's position did not offer the same opportunities to the attackers as did the avenues of Ronson, Green Finger and Warsaw. Caught in a ferocious concentration of artillery, tank and machine-gun fire, the Chinese suffered the most appalling casualties. Only six of them got as far as the wire in front of the trenches and within a matter of minutes the attack crumbled and faded out.

Having failed to consolidate their gains on the Hook and hurled two companies to destruction on Pt 121, the Chinese now switched their attention to Pt 146, where two companies of Kingsmen were waiting for them. For the second time that night

Mao's men were caught in the open. As soon as the Chinese were spotted forming up in front of Pheasant, the King's Commanding Officer, Lieutenant-Colonel Archie Snodgrass, called for artillery support. Heavy fire was brought to bear and no attack materialized. (Subsequently it was learned that a complete Chinese battalion had been caught by the guns and all but wiped out.) On Yong Dong the Black Watch had a grandstand view of this phase of the battle. The relative quietude of 'The Dong' was broken that night by several hundred shells – including a large number of British air bursts prematurely detonated in the rain clouds. By great good fortune, however, the Jocks suffered only one minor casualty in the battle.

The final attack was launched against the Hook at half-past midnight on the morning of 29 May. This time the Chinese attempted a lateral aproach from the feature Betty Grable in front of Pt 121. Ninety men charged north towards Ronson, and as they moved directly in front of Pt 121 they were caught not only in an artillery and mortar concentration which moved with them but by the machine-guns of Firth's composite company on Pt 121 and the Assault Pioneers on the ridge between Pt 121 and the Hook. Like the previous sally against Pt 121 this attack never stood a chance. How many Chinese remained alive when it was called off will never be known. But thirty bodies of men who participated in the assault were counted on the wire next morning.

Meantime the Dukes had set about recovering the ground they had lost on top of the Hook. Sherratt had not got very far towards the organization of a private counter-attack. Driven to shelter by the incessant shelling, he was apprehensive when he heard voices coming towards him. The Dukes had a nightly password, but he had forgotten it. So, when he heard the copulative adjective which distinguishes British troops, he shouted 'Dukes! Dukes!' His first cries were answered by a shot but he persisted until mutual recognition was finally established. 'I've found that captain from 'D' Company, and he's all right,' Sherratt heard one soldier announce. Then Campbell-Lamerton pushed his way forward 'Six foot four and a half and 17 and a half stone of rugger solidarity.' 'My God! I'm glad to see you,' said Sherratt, staring at another of the Dukes' rugger International.

Both Michael Campbell-Lamerton and David Gilbert-Smith were on their way to report to Emett as the first instalment of the reinforcements he had been clamouring for. As Sherratt ushered them into 'D' Company command post, Emett greeted him with 'Where the hell have you been?'

The plan to mop up the Chinese still holding the forward trenches was settled about 11.45 pm. Before the Yorkshiremen started on the actual clearance operation Ingram would fire three Verey lights – green over red over green. The knowledge of this signal, recognized as the Chinese code signal for a withdrawal, had been kept for just such a situation as this. When Ingram fired the signal, the gunners' 'Iron Ring' would be repeated, and the Dukes' counter-attack would follow. If all went according to plan, Campbell-Lamerton's men would then move into Dasent's area and Kirk's old positions would be cleared in a concerted pincer movement in which Ingram would function as the left claw and Gilbert-Smith as the right. In the event, when it came to putting this phase of the plan into operation, however, practical difficulties showed it to be unworkable. The whole of the top of the hill had literally changed shape, with rubble and tangled wire preventing any forward movement by Ingram's men – let alone working round towards Kirk's positions in the dark. With the right claw it was enemy fire which compelled a revision of Gilbert-Smith's role. When a crump of mortar bombs straddled his forward section, knocking out every single man, it was time to revise the way the operation should be conducted. In effect this meant resorting to a methodical advance up the line of the original trenches, necessarily a painfully slow business. Nevertheless, by 2 am Gilbert-Smith was able to report that he had reached the site of the bunker at the furthermost limit of the trench system. But there the devastation, rather than Chinese hazards, precluded any further progress before daylight.

Clearing Dasent's area proved to be a more tractable operation, and at 3.30 am an exhilarated Emett reported to Bunbury that the Hook was finally back in the Dukes' hands. *Virtutis fortuna comes*: Fortune had indeed favoured the Brave.

IO

THE OPENING OF THE TOMBS

Man cannot tell, but Allah knows
How much the other side was hurt!

KIPLING

At dawn on 29 May the full extent of the devastation on the Hook was revealed. Ten thousand Chinese shells had ploughed six-foot furrows in the terrain and levelled it like a well-worn football pitch. Trenches, which less than twenty-four hours before were eight foot six inches deep, had been smashed in and were now scarcely more than knee high; weapon pits had ceased to exist and the bunkers where men had lived were filled with rubble. Shredded sandbags and tangled bundles of barbed wire littered the area.

'Our wire,' wrote John Stacpoole, 'had played an important part in the battle, so I heard. The artillery barrage before the assault had chewed it up into a more than ever spiky tangle, tossing a lot of it into our partially destroyed trenches, so that the fighting bunkers and tunnels were sealed off from ready communication. We did not need to use those trenches, but only sit tight: the Chinamen wanted to use our trenches, but found them blocked by rubble and wire – those of them who were not caught enmeshed in the wire on top as we brought down VT shells like steel rain onto them.'

Among the debris the grisly remains of Chinese soldiers testified to the murderous effect of this steel rain. In the dull grey early morning light the scene rivalled that of the most gruesome illustrations of Dante's inferno. Chinese casualties were estimated at 250 dead, and 800 wounded; the Dukes suffered 149 casualties of whom 28 were killed. Sixteen men who were taken prisoner during the action were released when the Armistice Pact was signed in July. Two who returned were Private Leslie Lewington and Private Trevor Evans. Both were badly wounded in the early stages of the attack, but it was ten days before they received any medical attention. Neither remembered much about the first few hours after their capture – except that they were ushered down Green Finger into one of the Chinese caves. Mercifully and miraculously they survived a nightmare stumble through the British barrage; later in the night they were tied down on bamboo litters and jogged across No Man's Land. Ten days jolting across country on stretchers or over rough tracks in the back of a horse-drawn cart elapsed before they came to a prison camp. And by this time both men's wounds were gangrenous. Lewington had a leg amputated, but Evans was more fortunate. Like their fellow prisoners both of them were assured that under the 'Volunteers' New Lenient Policy they would not be murdered, tortured or have their personal belongings taken. During their stay as guests of the Chinese Peoples Republic they would enjoy the communist way of life. 'Everybody here is the same,' they were told. 'No officers, no NCOs here. Everybody is equal.' Luckily the Dukes' men did not have to 'enjoy' the communist standards of equality, food, crowded living conditions, and disease for very long.

A digging-out operation to free the men trapped in the Hook tunnels was mounted as soon as it was light. The battle had receded, and for a couple of hours the Chinese restricted their shelling to an occasional stonk. After the interminable din the silences seemed almost ghostly. The relief was immense – like the cessation of a dentist's drill after a long and painful boring of a cavity in a tooth. Then the guns opened up again.

Under the cover of a smoke screen, Sappers of 55 Squadron

Royal Engineers, under command of the moustachioed and lugubrious Captain Tom Watling, and battle-weary Dukes laboured to open up the tunnels, clear the debris, and patch up the defence in readiness for another assault. Private Husband came out fighting. 'Let me get at those f—— Chinks again,' he demanded. Kershaw was less belligerent. Release for him was the beginning of months of agonizing pain, culminating in the amputation of a foot. But he remained cheerful, and his first whispered query to Ernest Mackie was 'Are the crown jewels OK, Doc?'

Taylor, picked up by the King's on Pt 146, was another of the casualties who passed through Mackie's hands that morning. Still dazed, he could barely recall the details of his experiences, and when it was suggested to Bunbury that a patrol be sent out to recover Glen's body, the Dukes' CO refused. According to Taylor, Glen had died in a minefield and it was impossible to pinpoint his precise location. Finding Glen and bringing him back would certainly hazard other men's lives.

Bunbury wanted nobody's life hazarded unnecessarily. Up on the Hook at first light, he had been appalled at the extent of the damage and the appearance of his tired grimy troops. After the battle of Waterloo the Duke of Wellington wrote to Lady Frances Shelley: 'Next to a battle lost, the greatest misery is a battle gained.' A hundred and thirty-eight years later Ramsay Bunbury's sentiments were identical to those which had prompted these words of his gallant predecessor. Only a select few witnessed his grief, but Bunbury was greatly saddened by what he saw that morning.

Brigadier Kendrew was also shaken by what he saw. 'My God, those Dukes,' he said. 'They were marvellous. In the whole of the last war I never knew anything like that bombardment. But they held the Hook, as I knew they would.' And Kendrew, with three DSOs to his credit, had had plenty of experience of tough fighting. The Dukes had done all and more than he had expected. But he would see that the strain of the battle was telling on them. Moreover many of their weapons had been smashed or buried. If the Chinese launched another attack that night the Dukes would be at a disadvantage. Better, he decided, to relieve them with fresh troops. And so, at noon on 29 May the Dukes were heartened to see long snakes of soldiers winding up the hills towards their positions. 'What the hell's been going on?' asked one Fusilier, when he saw the mess. 'Just been seeing off a few Chinks,' replied one of the Dukes.

At 7.30 am I received orders that my battalion, the 1st Battalion, Royal Fusiliers, was to relieve the Dukes by noon. . . Hitherto relief in the line had always been conducted at night, with ample time for reconnaissance. . . Now, not only had the procedure to be speeded up but all movement had to take place in daylight – some of it in full view of the enemy.

The dirty end of the stick, the Hook feature, was given to 'A' Company, commanded by Major Henry Hill, a solid, stolid and most cheery officer. As a result of the heavy fighting of the night before the area was a complete shambles with almost every trench and bunker destroyed and all over-head cover and barbed wire utterly useless. The immediate priority was to get the defences and over-head cover restored as quickly as possible. 55 Field Squadron RE was allotted to help in this task and did most valiant work over the next few days. 'C' Company, the reserve company, provided working parties for the Hook area.

On the left of the Hook feature 'D' Company took over from a company of 1DWR on Pt 121, and on the right 'B' Company occupied 'The Sausage'. While all these reliefs were taking place there was constant shelling and mortaring of the positions. 'B' Company HQ had six men wounded by mortar bomb soon after they arrived in their area and there were other casualties. Despite this interference the relief was carried out according to plan and most of the Dukes were able to withdraw to rest. In addition to the generous help given by Ramsay Bunbury's men during the relief a nucleus was left behind to advise the new arrivals during their first night in a strange position.

Ramsay Bunbury remained at the command post for the night of

29/30 May to help me. I resisted a suggestion to move the command post because its location was probably known to the enemy. I doubted my ability to get a new one established in time to fight a battle that night and felt that forward troops would be unimpressed if my battalion headquarters moved, even sideways!

There was a good deal of tension that first night as standing patrols gave warnings of enemy movement and there were bursts of fairly heavy shelling. Several times we called for defensive fire from our own gunners. But, in the cold dark hours of the early morning, things quietened down and I managed to snatch a little sleep before going round the battalion position at dawn stand-to.

Thanks to the help of the Sappers the defences, the wire and the strength of the bunkers were quickly restored. A curious tower-like construction in 'A' Company's position drew scorn from the CRE but seemed to give the occupants comfort and satisfaction. For several nights there were alarms and excursions, many patrol clashes and warnings of possible enemy attacks. There were periods of heavy shelling from time to time. Whenever we saw the enemy we shelled and mortared them and sent out patrols to sweep the area. There was a steady drain of casualties, especially among officers, on account of the shelling and mortaring. One morning my jeep was hit just after I had left it to visit the Hook company, and my driver was wounded. But in time the enemy seemed to cease his aggressive tactics and our patrols began to report "NTR".

And so we slipped into the more normal routine of resting by day and keeping on our toes at night. On our left a section of 'D' Company shared a post with a Turkish section, friendly co-operation seemed to remove any language barrier. When the Turkish Battalion Commander visited my command post he greeted me: "We soldiers are only happy when we are fighting". I was not so sure.'[1]

For the Dukes the end of the battle on the Hook became synonymous with the end of the war, though in fact some weeks elapsed before the armistice agreement was signed at Panmun-

[1] Extract from a letter to the author from Colonel G. R. Stevens OBE.

jom. The attack for which Kendrew had thrust the Royal Fusiliers into the line never materialized. The Chinese had suffered such a set-back at the hands of the Dukes that they were in no position to mount another assault. But they were still occupying the Warsaw and Green Finger caves, and as this constituted an ever-present threat Kendrew decided to destroy the caves.

The operation was entrusted to the King's and at 10.30 pm, on a pitch dark night three strong fighting patrols sallied out down Long Finger. The operation had been carefully rehearsed and the men concerned were well-trained and keen; so what happened must largely be attributed to bad luck. Halfway towards their objective the leading patrol ran into an unanticipated tangle of wire which channelled them directly into a minefield. With three men killed and twelve wounded, all three patrols had to regroup in the middle of No Man's Land and the plan for the assault changed. Then, when a reformed raiding party resumed the advance towards the caves, the Chinese were waiting. As the Kingsmen charged up the Green Finger slope the re-entrant started to hum like a disturbed hornets' nest, and within minutes only three of the raiders were left unwounded. These three managed to blow up one of the caves, but the operation had virtually fizzled out already. Thirty-one casualties were suffered to little purpose. In victory there is some mitigation to such losses, but in defeat there is none – only remorse. To the victorious defensive battle this operation was a disappointing postscript. But it was not disastrous, and it did not detract from what General West described as 'a resounding victory, won by the inspiring gallantry of our men'.

EPILOGUE

This story has focused on a single action fought by one famous British infantry regiment on a barren lump of unmemorable ground. Many other regiments served in Korea and fought countless engagements which never got into the newspapers – little battles whose only historians were the casualty telegrams. The Dukes were the ones who held the hill on the night of 28/29 May, 1953, but they would be the first to pay tribute to those who made their victory possible – their predecessors, the sappers and above all the gunners.

Between sixty and eighty per cent of all these men were National Service conscripts, and no praise can be too high for them. Regular soldiers constituted the backbone of units like the Dukes, but it was the enthusiasm, discipline and general military efficiency of the National Servicemen which held the Hook. At the beginning of a new Elizabethan age they showed that Englishmen were the same as their forebears in the first age of Queen Elizabeth. In conditions of extreme hardship they behaved magnificently. The dirt and fatigue in Korea could not of course be compared to that experienced by those who served in Flanders during the First World War. Nor in the winter months was the exposure anything like that suffered by the armies in the Crimea during the nineteenth century. The services in the rear and the unending stream of good things which came up the lines of communication eased the lot of the soldiers in Korea. But for these highly organized supply lines, they would have suffered greater hardships than did the men who fought at Alma, Balaclava and Inkerman, because the demands of the 20th century soldier are far greater than those of his predecessors.

In one respect, however, it is questionable whether Britain treated her fighting men as generously as they deserved. The pay differential which existed between National Servicemen and Regulars was a constant irritation. Moreover even the highest rates of pay seemed inadequate in comparison with those of other Commonwealth troops and American G.I.s. As holidays are to a schoolboy, leave is to the soldier, and in wartime it is the brightest spot in his life. But at the leave camps in dollar-inflated Tokyo the British soldier soon found that his pay did not go very far. In Korea where there was little to spend money on the disparity in pay did not excite much bitterness. But at the Commonwealth Division's leave camp at Ebisu, where the British soldier saw Canadians, Australians and New Zealanders handling five, six and seven times as much money as he had been able to save, it constituted a real grievance.[1]

Whether British soldiers will ever fight another defensive battle like that of the Hook seems extremely doubtful. It is always difficult to discern what form future wars will take – at least the pundits have not been particularly successful in doing so in the past. But in the menacing shadow of nuclear might, the lavish means of defence available to the Dukes will be unlikely to exist. The possibility of devastating attacks on ports and concentrations of stores and materials will severely curtail the supply of ammunition essential to the build-up of a position like that established on the Hook. More than 37,000 British shells, 10,000 mortar bombs and half a million rounds of small arms ammunition were fired during the Third Battle of the Hook; for

---

[1] The National Serviceman's pay began at £1.25 (25 shillings) a week, rising after six months to £1.62 (32s. 6d.) and settled after 18 months service at £2.82 (£2 16s. 2d.) – provided he passed various tests. The New Zealand private soldier collected .87 NP (17s. 3d.) per day, the Australian more than £1.50 (30s.) per day and the Canadian still more.

seven hours one American gun fired an illuminating flare costing some £50 a time every two minutes, wearing out an expensive gun barrel in the process. Clearly, in the face of a nuclear threat such a prodigious expenditure of ammunition will be impossible. Nor is it likely that transport will be available to shift the enormous quantities of rations and other stores up to the front. Luxuries will be few and far between, and the infantry's morale will not be stimulated by beer, welfare, and NAAFI organizations, however admirable these things are. In a war for survival the troops will probably have to fight without their beer, chocolates and cigarettes. And because the Asiatic soldier – be he Chinese, Japanese, North Korean or Russian – is accustomed to exist and fight hard on a ration scale which makes that of the British Army look like a six course banquet, their fighting efficiency is less likely to be impaired. Since Korea, efforts have been made to streamline the fighting organization of the armies of the Western Powers. Judging by the performance of the American troops in Vietnam, the pruning process has not achieved a great deal in the US Army.

So far as the real effects of nuclear warfare are concerned, these can only be surmised. Much has been written about their devastating lethality, and it would be absurd to belittle the radical impact they will have on a battle. The defences and defenders of the Hook, for instance, could have been pulverized with a single atomic bomb. But it is as well to remember that massed destruction of human beings has not won tactical victory in the past. The Germans used phosgene gas in the First World War in an attempt to drive through to the English Channel, and British casualties were enormous. Yet neither that nor the massed employment of the killing power of artillery in the same war – on a hitherto unprecedented scale – produced more than local gains. The weight of Bomber Command in the battle east of Caen in July, 1944, did not by itself produce decisive results. In all these cases there were, of course, other important contributory causes, but other contributory causes always will exist.

What remains when it comes to the crunch is the critical element of human qualities. And in spite of all modern developments, it is still the infantry which plays the vital role. It is the infantry who guards the front; the front crumbles when the infantry crumble, and the front holds when the infantry hold.

Any nation can produce infantry of a sort, but it takes time and much devotion to produce the sort of infantry which which the British have produced such astonishing results with such relatively small numbers over several centuries. The secret of this success has been the regimental system built up on geographical loyalties, proud tradition and customs, and a measure of father-to-son sequence. Time after time on many isolated battlefields, in isolated platoon actions, the spirit generated by regimental *esprit de corps* has proved to be a battle-winning factor. Any infantry can fight for a certain length of time, but the infantry that can fight for even two minutes longer than their opponents win the day. Weapons and training are not enough. At the crucial stages of any action the infantry who have the most pride of regiment will get the upper hand. This pride, which resides in the officers and NCOs who have been brought up in its reflection, is quickly passed on to the soldiers.

Other nations have different methods of incentive. The Americans rely mainly on patriotism and overwhelming masses of material. The Israelis also have their burning patriotism. The Chinese rely on their own particular brand of communism, but the Russians, on top of their ideological training, put a great deal of faith in a form of regimental system.

During the Third Battle of the Hook pride of regiment sustained the Dukes, supplying the staying power and flame with which the Chinese were defeated. If, in these days of crumbling standards, any up-to-date proof of the need for some special inner discipline were needed to justify the British Army's proud tradition, their behaviour in this action will suffice.

APPENDIX A

THE INFANTRY BATTALION

A British infantry battalion is a self-contained unit with complex organization and equipment, intended 'with the support of other arms, to close with and destroy the enemy'. At the time of the Korean War both organization and equipment were virtually the same as in 1945. Since then, technological progress has forced changes in equipment and these, in turn, have led to changes in organization. For this reason a brief review of the component parts of the battalion and their capabilities *circa* 1953 seems justified.

1. Outline Organization

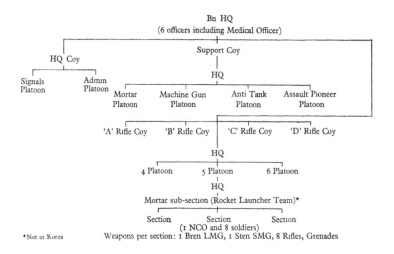

Summary of Personnel, Vehicles and Weapons

| | PERSONNEL | | VEHICLES | | WEAPONS | | |
	OFFRS	ORS		MMG	LMG	3″ MOR	2″ MOR
BN HQ	6	55	9		I		
HQ COY	5	145	22		6		
SP COY	6	164	38	6	16		6
RIFLE COY (× 4) 5		127	4		11	6	4
TOTAL	37	872	85	6	67	6	22

2. *Battalion Headquarters*

Battalion Headquarters comprised three main groups:

(a) The command element, including commanding officer, second-in-command, adjutant, assistant adjutant and police.

(b) The intelligence section and battalion snipers under the intelligence officer.

(c) The medical element.

3. *Command Element*

(a) *Second-in-command*

In Korea the duties of the second-in-command varied with different battalions and depended on personalities. The following were considered to be his normal duties:

(i) *During battle.* He was supposed to live with A Echelon, keeping in touch with Bn HQ by wireless and frequent visits to Bn HQ (the tactical Command Post). In the event, the peculiar conditions attached to the static warfare of Korea usually led to the 2 i/c living and working alongside the CO at the CP.

(ii) *During Rest Periods.* Theoretically he was responsible for training. In fact very few COs were prepared wholeheartedly to delegate the responsibility.

(b) *Adjutant.* He is – and was – the 'G' and 'A' staff officer to the CO. In battle he remained with battalion HQ, allowing the CO to roam at will.

(c) *Assistant adjutant.* Relieved the adjutant of work unconnected with operations. He was usually left out of battle and worked at either 'A' or 'B' echelon.

(d) *Intelligence Officer.* Controlled the intelligence section and snipers. (Ramsay Bunbury's choice of a WO2 at IO was an instance of his determination to fit a round peg in a round hole.)

(e) *Regimental Sergeant-major.* In action the RSM dealt with ammunition supply and controlled the regimental police. He also organized concealment and the defence of battalion HQ.

(f) *Provost.* Strength one sergeant and four regimental police. Duties included signposting routes and traffic control.

4. *Intelligence Section*

(a) *Organization.* Strength one sergeant, one corporal and two privates. (According to the official notes on this subject the 'I' section personnel should be 'well educated and include any draughtsmen or linguists in the unit.')

(b) *Employment.* Collecting, collating and passing on information on enemy activity and the ground; man OPs. Also dealt with maps and air photographs.

(c) *Snipers*

(i) *Organization.* Under control of the intelligence officer. Strength one Warrant Officer Class II (who in many units combined these duties with those of Weapon Training Instructor) and six privates from the Corps of Drums (HQ Coy) who were trained as snipers.

(ii) *Employment.* Specially trained expert shots armed with telescopic-sighted rifles; used in pairs to observe and harass the enemy and to deny him close observation of the battalion position.

5. *Medical*

(a) *Organization*

(i) *RAMC.* One medical officer, one sergeant and five corporals (attached).

(ii) *Infantry.* One sergeant and 20 stretcher bearers one of whom was a corporal.

(b) *Employment.* At the regimental aid post. Responsible for the collection and evacuation of all wounded in the battalion area. Stretcher-bearers were attached to rifle companies as required.

6. *Headquarter Company,* which consisted of a Corps HQ, the Signal platoon and an Administrative platoon was commanded by a major, who in battle normally commanded 'B' echelon transport.

7. *Signal Platoon.* This was organized into two sections: the wireless section and the Signal office and line section. Its task was to provide wireless, line and despatch rider communication within the battalion. In the static warfare scenario line provided the backbone of the communication, but this was quickly knocked out when the Hook battle started.

Equipment:

(i) *Wireless* No 62 sets   4

            No 31 sets   18 plus 4 replacement sets

            No 88 sets   26 plus 1 replacement set

(ii) *Line:* Officially   10 2/3 miles D3 or D9 cable

                 15 miles assault cable

                 3 10-line magnetic telephone exchanges

                 36 telephones which permitted party line in each coy consisting of company HQ and three platoon HQ. In practice more line equipment was used.

Wireless sets. It should be noted that a No 62 set was able to work to a No 19 set.

8. *Administrative Platoon.* Consisted of the battalion transport officer and his staff, and the battalion quartermaster and his staff (which included the tradesmen pioneer section). Also the Drum Major, and 16 drummers or pipers who were deployed for the close defence of battalion HQ, and 6 of whom were trained as battalion snipers.

(a) *Battalion Transport Officer.* Assisted by his technical staff he supervised maintenance of mechanical transport and dealt with unit repairs.

(b) *Battalion Quartermaster.* Responsible for all supplies and stores (except technical). Commodities were carried as follows:

(i) *Rations and Cooking.* One 5-ton truck and one 1-ton trailer to each rifle company and one 3-ton truck and one 1-ton trailer shared between Headquarter Company and Support Company: each could carry company quartermaster sergeant and ACC cooks, company cooking set, unconsumed portion of day's ration, and a proportion of the battalion reserve rations.

(ii) *Water.* One 1-ton truck (200 gallons) and one 1-ton trailer (180 gallons). The truck driver was trained in water duties.

(iii) *Petrol*. One 3-ton truck used for the supply of petrol, oil and lubricants. The driver was trained as a petrol store-man.

(iv) *Ammunition*. Two 3-ton trucks carried the battalion reserve ammunition. The Regimental Sergeant Major's 1-ton truck and trailer in Battalion Headquarters carried a futher reserve.

(c) *Tradesmen*. In theory it was the tradesmen pioneer section which was responsible for:

(i) The construction of shelters, dug-outs and command posts.

(ii) The improvement of buildings for defence.

(iii) The setting up of a simple waterpoint to supplement water trucks.

In practice much of the work on shelters and dug-outs was carried out by men from the rifle companies (in their own areas) and the Assault Pioneer Platoon.

(d) *Special dutymen*

(i) Sanitary dutymen were also trained in water duties.

(ii) Two drivers in the administrative platoon and one in each rifle company were trained as equipment repairers.

9. *Support Company*. This comprised company HQ, mortar platoon, MG platoon, anti-tank platoon and assault pioneer platoon. Elements of the support company could be sub-allotted to companies to assist companies in carrying out their tasks, but conditions in Korea tended towards centralization. OC Support Company did not usually receive orders from the CO for the deployment of his platoons, but he administered them and, of course, he supervised their training.

10. *Mortar Platoon*

(a) *Organization*. Platoon HQ and three sections of two 3-inch mortars.

(b) *Employment*. These mortars constituted a battalion's own close support weapon. They could fire high explosive or smoke bombs. They possessed a very high rate of fire so that the quantity of ammunition and not number of mortars available was the key to the volume of fire.

(c) *Handling*. The mortar platoon was able to fire from the map or from scaled air photographs without observation. Mortars can be manhandled by crews over long distances, but to make this worthwhile a considerable number of men were required from outside the platoon to carry ammunition. This requirement was filled by Korean porters.

11. *Machine Gun Platoon*
   (a) *Organization.* Platoon HQ and three medium machine gun sections (each two medium machine guns). All were carried in $\frac{1}{4}$-ton trucks (three per section).
   (b) *Employment.* In Korea medium machine gun sections fought dismounted. The chief characteristics of the platoon were the extent of their fire power and mobility. Their tasks included:
      (i) Covering the front of and gaps between localities and protecting exposed flanks.
      (ii) Providing a mobile reserve of hard-hitting small arms fire.
      (iii) Delaying the enemy.
      (iv) Assisting local counter attacks.
      (v) Providing harassing fire.
   In Korea the DWR's MGs were used mainly for map shooting (indirect) fire at night. Some 50 pre-recorded DF/MG tasks were included in the Hook defensive fire plan. The Vickers guns used the same techniques as the artillery to fire on map reference targets – but with even greater problems of safety and crest clearance. During the third battle of the Hook prerecorded map reference targets were supplemented by requests for non-recorded map reference shoots which were worked out from scratch.
   (c) The wasp section that formed part of the MG platoon during the later stage of the 2nd World War had been abolished. In Korea there was little use for a flame throwing vehicle.

12. *Anti-tank Platoon*
   This platoon was not used in Korea.
   (a) *Organization.* Platoon HQ, six detachments, each of one 17 pounder gun, for which there was no use in the Korean hills.[1] Some battalions retained the platoon as a battalion headquarters defence platoon. Others, like the Dukes, put it into suspended animation.
   (b) *Employment.* In countries where tanks operated its primary task was to destroy enemy armour trying to penetrate into the

[1] In Europe the recoilless anti-tank gun, the BAT, was being introduced about this time.

156

battalion area. (Mention has been made of the Anti-tank platoon to complete the picture.)

13. *Assault Pioneer Platoon*
 (a) *Organization.* Platoon HQ, and three assault sections (each one NCO and eight pioneers).
 (b) *Employment.* The platoon was expected to be capable of:
   (i) Reconnoitring mined areas.
   (ii) Clearing lanes through mined areas.
   (iii) Laying, arming, neutralizing and lifting all types of mines, and teaching others the procedures involved.
   (iv) Clearing mines when necessary.
   (v) Setting and neutralizing booby traps.
   (vi) Bunker-building, tunnelling, trench-revetting, rock-blasting, wiring and field defences.
   (vii) Using the equipment of the assault platoon of the Bridge Company RASC.
   (viii) Advising on knots and lashing.
   (ix) Making elementary use of explosives in connection with field defences and destruction of enemy equipment.
   (x) Preparing assault demolitions and cratering.
 (c) *Equipment.* In addition to other stores the platoon held: prodders for detecting mines, mine detectors and demolition charges.

14. *Rifle Companies* (Four)
 (a) *Organization.* Company HQ and three platoons, each of platoon HQ, mortar sub-section, Rocket Launcher Team and three sections.
 (b) *Employment.* The rifle companies were the basic infantry whose job it was to close with the enemy and finally force the decision by their physical presence on the ground.
 (c) *Weapons.* The weapons of the rifle coy gave:
   (i) Assaulting power – rifles and bayonets.
   (ii) Covering fire – IMGs and 2-in or 60-mm mortars.
   (iii) Close quarter fighting power – SMGs (Sten machine carbines), pistols, grenades and bayonets.
   (iv) Anti-tank protection (not in Korea).
   This array of weapons, of which every infantry man was required to be a master, made the infantry a highly specialized team.

157

15. *Reinforcements and Left out of Battle Personnel*

Certain personnel were normally left out of battle before a major attack. There was no laid down scale and numbers were adjusted according to battalion strengths and the availability of reinforcements held in the Commonwealth Divisional unit.

16. *Equipment*

The scale of a battalion's equipment, laid down in June, 1950, was increased during the Korean war.

(a) The weight a man can carry affects his fighting efficiency, and it was decided that 50–55 pounds was the limit for battle order.

(b) Every man required to operate some new device decreased the strength of rifle companies assaulting power.

17. *Clothing and Personal Equipment*

It would be true to say that no army has ever been better clothed. In the cold weather there was little trench foot and few cases of frostbite. Long underpants, string vests, windproof suits and outer parkas generated warmth.

The armoured waistcoat, an innovation of the Korean War, was issued on a scale of 60 per rifle company and it is credited with the saving of lives. Though it has been criticized since, it appeared to be proof against Burp gun bullets at ranges beyond 30 yards; even at close ranges the protection it gave reduced the lethality of the latter.

18. *Weapons*

The performance of the Sten gun was shown to be inadequate and, of course, it was due for replacement by the L2AI SMG. The need for a self-loading rifle was also apparent although the well tried No 4 Rifle served its purpose. The 3 inch mortars were excellent, but the 2 inch mortar failed because it was inaccurate, had insufficient range and no reliable illuminating flare.

APPENDIX B

CHINESE TACTICS IN KOREA 1952-1953

In the static warfare period the Chinese used their huge manpower resources, skilled and unskilled alike, to produce a formidable defensive system to seal off North Korea. They were not allowed to build this defensive line free from molestation, and considerable punishment was inflicted in the process. But the Chinaman is both patient and persistent. And nightly he set out to mend the damage inflicted by day by the U.N. Air Force and U.N. artillery. What he was able to accomplish may serve as a reminder that the days of intensive and extensive positional warfare in defence may not be so outmoded as the lessons of the Second World War have suggested. It is certainly a lesson in what can be done with manpower alone, given a sufficient quantity of it, with picks and shovels, a few crowbars, a little explosive, some ingenuity and a great deal of hard work.

1. *The Defence Line*

In this period the distance between the Chinese front line and that of the U.N. troops was usually governed by the distance between adjacent hills – anything from 300 to 1000 yards apart. In general the U.N. troops occupied the hill tops and forward slopes by day and night; the Chinese occupied them only by night. By day they kept to the reverse slopes.

In some places distances between the two front lines were further apart, with one or two hills in No Man's Land – unoccupied by either side but patrolled by both sides at night. Occasionally in Central Korea they were much closer together. Indeed in one place the opposing trenches were only about thirty yards apart, and the U.S. troops occupying the U.N. line erected wire netting to ward off grenades. This situation was exceptional, but the fact remains that trench warfare in Korea often exceeded in extent and intensity the trench warfare of the First World War.

After November, 1951, the front line was static. The U.N. air force was virtually unopposed over the forward areas, and together with the U.N. artillery was capable of inflicting heavy casualties whenever the Chinese troops moved in the open by day. Thus in order to keep alive they were forced to get underground by day. In the later stages of the truce negotiations they may also have believed that they might have to face a nuclear attack.

In the course of six months the Chinese developed a sketchy front line into a system of well-sited and well-constructed strong points. To withstand U.N. artillery and air bombardment, emplacements were built with strong overhead protection, proof against anything but infantry assault or a direct hit from a 500-lb bomb.

The peaks, ridges and dominant features of the hills formed the basis of the Chinese defence line. Company and battalion strong points were deployed in depth in all round fortifications. Each of these positions consisted of mutually supporting rifle, machine-gun, mortar and artillery points connected by a network of communication trenches. All were provided with deep underground shelters and ammunition stores, so that the Chinese were able to live for long periods without exposing themselves to observation or fire.

Local timber was used to reinforce positions dug into the ground and logs were used to increase the strength of the overhead protection. unlike the U.N. troops little use was made of sandbags – presumably because they were not available. All the positions were carefully camouflaged with bushes and turf, making them extremely difficult to spot from the air.

Each strong point usually had a communication trench following the contour of the hill. This often had heavy overhead protection on the forward slope and sometimes on the reverse slope also. Branching off from this main communication trench were connecting trenches leading to weapon pits and shelters. Some of these had overhead protection and between positions on the forward and reverse slope there were often tunnels. The trenches were 5 to 6 feet deep and 2 feet wide, with 3 to 6 feet of earth and logs on top. The tunnels were about 2 feet wide and 3 feet high; where the earth was soft they were shored up with timber.

Individual rifle positions, cut into the main communication trenches on both the forward and reverse slopes, usually did not have overhead cover. But in less well-developed parts of the line, lacking covered communication trenches, individual rifle pits were covered in. Machine-guns were usually dug in near the crest of a hill, and protected by 3 to 6 feet of earth. Mortar emplacements were usually sited on the reverse slopes to cover ground dead to flat trajectory weapons dug in about 4 feet and provided with overhead cover similar to that given to machine-guns. Mortar Observation Points were usually linked to the emplacements by a tunnel.

Troops shelters were incorporated in the strong point systems. These were constructed on the reverse slopes with very strong overhead protection of anything up to 12 feet of earth. Others were dug deep into the sides of hills with access by tunnel. Logs of up to 12 inches in diameter were used to support the roof and the shelters were capable of standing up to any bombardment less than a direct hit from a 500-lb bomb. Most of them provided space for five men only, so that casualties were reduced if any single shelter received a direct hit. None were more than 5 feet high and they were often provided with the 'chuffer' type of heaters similar to those used by U.N. troops.

In the last year of the war the Chinese dug and camouflaged emplacements for their artillery. Usually a tunnel allowed the gun to be pulled into a protected emplacement for firing; when not in action the gun could then be pulled back to safety. Gun crews' quarters and ammunition stores were dug in near the gun and protected equally with the weapon.

The Chinese made little use of concrete and they appear to have had very little wire. This was probably due as much to the problems of transporting it forward as to shortage of supply. Nor did they sow minefields to the same extent as the U.N. forces. Fenced off and marked minebelts were not a feature of their defensive layout, but on occasions they did lay a few concealed mines on the routes used by U.N. patrols. However they were extremely skilful at making improvised booby traps from shells, grenades and explosive charges.

2. *Tactics*

While the negotiations at Panmunjom dragged on the Chinese did not become Maginot-minded. They remained alert, their patrols were aggressive and their artillery and mortar fire was well directed. They probed the U.N. front continuously and whenever there seemed to be an opportunity to exploit a weakness they took it. Constantly they sought to seize key positions, which would be militarily advantageous if the negotiations broke down. The tempo of the deadly fighting for features like The Hook remained unchanged until the end. By that time their techniques had improved – especially their ability to mass and shift artillery fire in support of infantry attacks. The attacks on The Hook were unsuccessful but they did show that the Chinese were well disciplined and that the quality of their junior leaders was high.

The pattern of the attacks – the probing and the standard 'one-point-two-sides' method developed by Lin Piao, and the 'three fierce actions' have been described in the text. Attacking formations ranged as a rule from a platoon to a company in size, being continually built up as casualties thinned the ranks. Newspaper reports of 'hordes' and 'human sea' assaults were unrealistic enough to inspire the comment by a U.S. Marine 'How many hordes are there in a Chinese platoon?'

Chinese tactics clearly deserve credit. Yet they had some serious weaknesses. If an attack failed, stocks of shells and mortar bombs needed to be replenished before it could be renewed, and here the primitive logistical system showed its limitations. There is a limit to what human and animal transport can carry by night. Some short-comings may also be attributed to the primitive communication system used by the Chinese. A radio net rarely extended below battalion level. From battalion to companies and platoons, communications depended on runners or bugles, whistles, flares and flash-lights. Because of this the assault tactics had to conform to a rigid pattern which at times was fatal. Chinese commanding officers had little or no option below battalion level, and a battalion once committed to an attack often kept on as long as its ammunition lasted – even if events indicated that it was beating its brains out. As has been seen on The Hook, the result in many cases was tactical suicide.

3. Logistics

Finally, because the need for 'cutting the tail' of the armies of the Western Powers is a popular topic some comparative figures are thought to be worthy of consideration.

In battle a Chinese first-line division consumed 40 to 50 short tons of supplies a day. This represents 8 to 10 lbs per man as compared to almost 60 lbs a man required to sustain an American Division and 50 lbs to sustain a British Division. Needless to say the Chinese did not provide their troops with the amenities their U.N. counterparts seemed to require. This basic tonnage was made up as follows:

19·2 tons Rations and Water
 8·8 tons Clothing and Equipment
 4·0 tons Fuel and Lubricants
 8·0 tons Ammunition
 ───
40·0 tons

When 50 tons could be delivered to divisional dumps, the excess 10 tons was dispersed in dugouts behind the front.

To supply a maximum of 50 front line and local reserve divisions, and to build up forward stockpiles, the Chinese needed to carry up no more than an average of 2500 short tons per day. In contrast, the Commonwealth Division carried about 600 tons per day. On a man-for-man basis (taking account of the relative 'bayonet' strength) the U.N. Command had to move to the front about 7 tons to each ton the Chinese moved.

SOURCES AND
ACKNOWLEDGEMENTS

The foundations of this book consist of eye-witness testimonies, supplied by many people.

The following books, Regimental Journals and newspapers have also been consulted:

1. *Books*

Barclay, Brigadier C. N., CBE, DSO   *The First Commonwealth Division*, Gale & Polden, Aldershot, 1954.

Carew, Tim   *Korea*, Cassell, London, 1967.

George, Alexander L.   *The Chinese Communist Army in Action*, Columbia University Press, New York, 1967.

Griffith, Samuel B.   *The Chinese People's Liberation Army*, McGraw-Hill, New York, 1967.

Hermes, Walter C.   *Truce Tent and Fighting Front*, Office of the Chief of Military History U.S. Army, Washington, 1966.

Howard, Philip   *The Black Watch*, Leo Cooper, London, 1968.

O'Ballance, Edgar   *Korea 1950–1953*, Faber & Faber, London, 1969.

2. *Regimental Journals*

The Kingsman
The Iron Duke
The Red Hackle

3. *Newspapers*

The Yorkshire Post and Leeds Mercury
The Yorkshire Evening Post
The Yorkshire Observer
The Middlesborough Evening Gazette
The Newcastle Journal
The Isle of Man Weekly Times
The Times
The Daily Telegraph
The Daily Express
The Sunday Express
The Daily Herald
The News Chronicle
The Daily Mirror

The number of people who went to considerable trouble to assist me is too great for individual mention, but some were particularly important. The idea of a book on the epic battle of The Hook originated with Dom Alberic Stacpoole, MC, now a monk at Ampleforth, who has prompted and eased my research, recreated the atmosphere and made the substantial contributions which are included and acknowledged in the text. To him I am especially grateful.

To His Excellency Major-General Sir Douglas Kendrew, KCMG, CB, CBE, DSO, Governor of Western Australia, I must express my thanks for assistance, criticism and, of course, the Foreword.

Others who produced contemporary evidence and who deserve special mention include: Major R. E. Austin, MC, Major B. W. R. Baker, Brigadier F. R. St P. Bunbury, CBE, DSO, Major E. J. P. Emett, MC, Brigadier A. D. Firth, OBE, MC, Major C. Grieve, Lieut.-Col. C. R. Huxtable, Colonel A. B. M. Kavanagh, OBE, MC, Lieut.-Col. A. M. Lamont, Lieut.-Col. H. S. LeMesurier, Dr. E. D. Mackie, James E. MacMillan, Lieut.-Col. E. W. Nicoll, Captain A. Robbins, MBE, Major W. F. C. Robertson, Lieut.-Col. D. Rose, DSO, Major R. A. Sherratt, Colonel G. R. Stevens, OBE, Col. the Rev. D. I. Strangeways, DSO, OBE, and CSM D. Taylor. The assistance provided by Mr Edwin R. Flatequal of the Department of the Chief of Military History, United States Army, is also gratefully acknowledged, and I should especially like to thank Mr Joe Avery for the facilities he provided for my wife and myself to examine the Korean War records in the U.S. National Records Center, Washington, DC.

The majority of those who offered to help did so because they took a keen professional interest in the battle and research had not proceeded very far before the author became aware that he was in good hands; recollections were very much more detailed and precise than might have been expected after a lapse of nearly twenty years. The reason was that the events were regarded as important by the witnesses, at the time and after, and therefore they were retained in the memory. Corporal 'Spud' Taylor for instance was unlikely to forget what happened to him on 29 May, 1953, and his narrative was still horrifyingly vivid. Absolute accuracy in describing any very rapid sequence of exciting events is, of course, impossible – even five seconds afterwards. The exact order of events sometimes becomes confused and the human brain cannot concentrate at full efficiency for much more than twenty minutes even in favourable conditions: weariness, cold and hunger all detract from efficiency. These limitations accepted, I believe that the present reconstruction of the battle is tolerably accurate, although for the final judgement, the verdict of the veterans will have to be awaited. I do not believe that there are any striking disagreements with official pronouncements, but for my own comments, of course, I bear sole responsibility.

A final word of thanks must go to my wife Alexandra, who has had to live on The Hook, typing and retyping a series of drafts, while the book was being born.

INDEX